WE HAVE A
GOOD TIME ...
DON'T WE?

Maeve Higgins studied photography in college and worked in a clothes shop until 2004. Then, one magical March evening, she discovered her dream life as a stand-up comedian. Since then she has written and performed various shows for comedy festivals all around the world. Maeve starred in RTÉ's *Naked Camera* and went on to make her own comedy series with her sister Lilly called *Fancy Vittles*, which was a cult hit. She lives in Dublin and has part ownership of a very gentle Alsatian. *We Have a Good Time . . . Don't We?* is her first book.

WE HAVE A
GOOD TIME ...
DON'T WE?

A Regular
Human Girl
Decides

MAEVE HIGGINS

HACHETTE
BOOKS
IRELAND

First published in 2012 by Hachette Books Ireland
A division of Hachette UK Ltd.

A CIP catalogue record for this title is available from the British Library.

ISBN 978 1 444 74340 1

Typeset and layout design by redrattledesign.com
Cover design by AmpVisual.com
Cover photo by Jeannie O'Brien
Inside illustration by Maeve Clancy

Printed and bound by CPI Group (UK) Ltd, Croydon, CR0 4YY
Hachette Books Ireland policy is to use papers that are natural, renewable and recyclable products and made from wood grown in sustainable forests. The logging and manufacturing processes are expected to conform to the environmental regulations of the country of origin.

Hachette Books Ireland
8 Castlecourt Centre
Castleknock
Dublin 15, Ireland

A division of Hachette UK Ltd
338 Euston Road
London NW1 3BH
www.hachette.ie

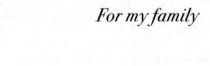

For my family

Contents

There's no shame in it:
my secrets

Do you have curly hair, or what? I can't figure it out.
I do. I have curly hair. I have a side fringe. A full fringe apparently makes my face look round. And nobody likes a round face. I keep telling babies that, but they insist on having full, sunny circles as faces and that's their prerogative. The ideal face shape is oblong. Anyway, I keep my side fringe dead straight. I never allow it to spring into its natural curls, as that makes me look like a woman waiting for her cousin-husband at a monster truck rally.

How do you get so many great guys?
I stand very close to them – uncomfortably close. When they finish talking, I laugh for a really long time while maintaining eye contact. That is like catnip to them.

What is your least appealing trait?
I get xenophobic and racist when I'm jet-lagged. I watch TV and think about how fat Americans are and what terrible soldiers Italians make. I get in a taxi and assume the Chinese driver doesn't know the way. I tell my English friend to keep

1

her voice down: that it's oppressive. When my melatonin rights itself, I'm straight back to my right-on self.

Who is your favourite sister? They all seem great – is it hard to choose? You have to.
This question, along with my financial situation, keeps me up at night. When we are all back home, I scrutinise my sisters one by one and in various combinations, but it's just too hard to pick a winner. I think maybe it's because I'm the best one, but I feel bad saying that!

What exactly is your financial situation?
Let's just say *somebody* has to get her career going, or else get married, very, very soon.

Who's Marjorie?
Marjorie is a mole on my foot, which my sister Daisy is afraid of.

Why are you nice to people you don't like?
Because I am scared of people not liking me, you dummy! Just joking – you're not a dummy. Your top is lovely.

In the bathroom, why do you sometimes run the tap but not actually wash your hands? If you don't need to wash your hands, there's no need to pretend to, surely? Do you want people who may be listening outside the door to think you have, is that it?
If I've put on my good hand cream earlier and have only

done a piddle, I don't see why I should ... Hang on! Who are you, and how do you know all of this stuff?

I am your mother.
MAMMY! You got me.

She likes human food, particularly butter

In her book *Down Came the Rain*, Brooke Shields writes movingly of having postnatal depression so badly that she imagines her baby sliding down a wall. I have to admit, I've imagined the same thing happening to my cat, Little Edie. I love her, but she really pushes my buttons. She is haughty and naughty, and basically moved next door last year. She just drops in through the cat flap every now and then, scares the dogs and has a bite to eat. She likes human food, particularly butter. I keep it in the fridge, not by choice, but because she's not tall enough or strong enough to open the fridge door yet. Once, I forgot, and left the butter on the counter top. When I came downstairs that afternoon, only half of it remained, licked smooth and misshapen, like a Dali clock. As I held the butter dish, bereft, I felt someone watching me. I looked out the window to my neighbour's garden. There was Little Edie, staring in at me. I opened the window and called her an asshole. I couldn't help it. She turned her head away slowly, in an incredibly controlled way – like I do when I'm caught staring at someone attractive.

In my darkest moments, I fear that she doesn't even like me. I got her from the shelter four years ago, as company for my main cat, Michael. He was a knockout: big and white and fluffy and clumsy. I'd cuddle him a lot, sometimes so hard, it surprised him and he would kind of wheeze. *Hush now, baby,* I'd whisper to him, *I didn't know how much I loved you either.* Despite my affection, Michael had itchy feet, and was forever darting out of my arms and escaping through windows. I thought he would settle down if he had a friend, but two months after I brought Little Edie home, he ran away for good. I look for him still, scanning crowds hopefully, like a war widow who never got a body.

After Michael left, Little Edie and I soon realised we didn't have much in common. I suppose she figured out that she was the spare cat, and because of the difficult start we had, we never bonded properly. Four years later, she still hates physical contact. I asked the vet if cats sometimes scratched as a form of play. He shook his head slowly as I showed him my forearms, covered in claw marks.

One day, in desperation, I Googled *Is my cat happy?* The internet told me that if a cat stares at you you then slowly opens and closes their eyes, that's their way of saying *I love you and I'm here for you.* You can return the favour and open and close your eyes slowly if you want, to boost your cat's self-esteem. Little Edie does stare at me, almost constantly, but rarely slow-blinks. In fact, she has a chilling propensity for unbroken eye contact. She seeks it out even when using her litter tray. I believe she holds on until she's locked eyes with a person. It's disconcerting for visitors.

Unnerving as she is, I really miss her when she's not around. When she lived with me full time, she would follow me from room to room, silently judging my actions. It was

5

like having a little physical manifestation of my conscience. I regularly felt the need to justify myself. *Come on … it's normal to spend the early hours of the morning making a mood-board of images of my head on the bodies of former members of Destiny's Child,* I'd hear myself say, and, *Don't look so disgusted, Little Edie, the dentist said you're supposed to smell the dental floss – it's how you tell whether or not you've got gum disease.*

In August of last year, my neighbour Mrs Douglas began feeding her. Mrs Douglas would ring a bell, one of those little bells you give an invalid trapped upstairs. Little Edie would wake up, stretch and bound out of the cat flap and in through Mrs Douglas's kitchen window. I monitored the situation for a few months, not saying anything to either of them, until I realised Little Edie hadn't spent a night at home in over two weeks.

Mrs Douglas is in her eighties. She lives alone and deserves mad props for that. I want to live alone one day too, but considering I still need somebody to tell me what to wear for meetings and when it's time for bed, I don't think I'm ready just yet. Every few weeks, Mrs Douglas and I meet up for tea in a café on our street. We avoid discussing the elephant in the room, which is my cat in her house. We talk about food instead. She says she likes plain food, like toast and potatoes. I say I like plain food too, but also fussy food like trifle. Mrs Douglas usually gets a scone and doesn't like the fact that I don't. Without fail, she offers me half of hers. I've told her a thousand times that I'm gluten intolerant, but old people generally don't believe that. Once she said, in a voice more raised than either of us expected: *Oh come on, Maeve, eat it for your Granny!* After that, we were both quiet for ages.

The only time we address the fact that she's stolen my cat is when we both happen to be in our gardens at the same time. We have had a number of passive-aggressive exchanges about the situation, across the hedge, while Mrs Douglas rubs the cat with her cane and Little Edie rolls around, thrilled with herself.

I say: *Oh. There's my cat! Wow. I guess she won't come home because you're feeding her that jelly stuff, even though the vet told me not to feed her that, because it's like McDonald's for cats – momentarily delicious but nutritionally pointless.*

Mrs Douglas replies: *But she really enjoys it and the poor little thing is always so hungry! And I don't mind the expense. She's gas altogether, always sitting on my lap. As soon as I sit down, she's up on my lap like a shot.*

I glare at the cat, who glares back at me, and I say: *Oh, she's a real lap cat. I don't know what I'd do without her – she's like my hot-water bottle.* That would be true, if I owned a hot-water bottle and it actively disliked me.

To be entirely honest, it's quite nice to see them together. Mrs Douglas hangs out the washing while Little Edie studies her intently. She puts out her rubbish into the back garden – the cat watches, fascinated. I'm worried Little Edie has imprinted on Mrs Douglas permanently, though, like the wolf boy everybody fancies from *Twilight*. That would mean I've lost her, and I can't afford to lose a second cat. It would be proof that I'm bad at being an adult.

I began a campaign to win her back. I combed through Dublin city's finest jewellers in search of a little bell of my own to entice her back to my house. Turns out, jewellers don't sell bells, but a number of them assured me that they do engrave them. I resorted to buying a crystal tumbler and dinging it out the window, with a silver spoon. And it worked. It sounds like a bell and I feel like a duchess doing it, but most importantly, it makes Little Edie come as far as the cat flap and sniff around. I have a bowl of the cheapest jellied cat food on the market, waiting to tempt her inside, and that's working too. She pads over to the bowl and eats in that biting way cats have. When she's finished, she looks into my hopeful eyes for a long moment. I close them slowly and open them just in time to see her walking away, into the dusk.

They're just poppers,
don't worry

In the 1980s, it was difficult to find building work in Ireland, so my father went to London to work. We children were preoccupied with thoughts of how lonely he must be over there. We wondered what he would eat and if people were pushing into him on the trains. He came home most weekends, and left on Monday mornings. Massive doom filled the house on Sunday nights. One child would start whimpering at the thought of him leaving, and quite quickly all hell would break loose, until my mother banned us from crying over him.

Instead, we invented a unique ritual for saying goodbye to him. On Monday mornings, whenever we heard a plane flying overhead, we would run out to the garden and hold up silver pots and pans, angling them against the light to create what we hoped were glinting goodbye kisses to one airborne David Higgins.

This seems implausibly adorable, so much so that, when I began to write about it here, I was worried I invented this memory, and phoned my mother to verify its accuracy. Trying to get hold of my mother on her mobile phone is almost impossible. The process mystifies her too much. I've watched her hold the phone as it rings out, wondering what to do. She does return calls on it, but only when it's impossible for her to talk.

Like in this case, when she called me back a few hours later and yelled down the phone: *Maeve, is that you? I'm down on the strand with the dogs and I can't hear you over the waves! I'll try you later on.* She put her phone into her pocket without hanging up.

That evening, she phoned again. I said *Hi!*, and she breathed: *Sshh. I'm at the community centre for a talk on beekeeping, but I can sort of whisper – I'm near the back* ... Then nothing. I assumed she'd dropped her phone into some honey.

I didn't hear from her until the following afternoon, and this time there were sounds of screaming and gunshots in the background. *Listen, I can't really talk, the party has literally just started – there are fifteen kids here and they're all off their heads* ...

It was my youngest foster sister's birthday party that afternoon. My mother was attempting to sound harried, but the children's party business is right up her alley – she's like a grizzled old boxer going up against a sparky rookie. It will always be tough for a few rounds, but her experience and tenacity as a fighter will outshine the youngster's wild swings and ensure her victory every time.

I really have to go – they're climbing on the fridge!

OK, OK – but what's that noise? Does someone have a gun?

They're just poppers, don't worry ... I tell her not to call them 'poppers', but she's gone, to dole out jelly and ice cream to a new batch of seven-year-olds.

Three days later, I get her in the relative quietness of the kitchen. I ask her if she can corroborate my memory of us children leaping around the garden, with saucepans aloft. She said yes, that we did that most Monday mornings for the best part of a year, and that the smaller ones among us would just hold up lids. She said we would quiz our father on the phone at night-time, asking him if the other passengers were jealous – worried we'd distracted the pilot. Daddy would assure us that seeing our signals made his trip much easier, because he knew we were thinking of him. Of course, he never saw us. Nobody ever saw us tiny, desperate lunatics except our mother, watching from the kitchen window, with a heart close to breaking.

A regular, human girl

Here's a cheap old stand-up comedy trick I'm going to let you in on. To guarantee a laugh, say something self-deprecating, then follow it up by talking about how you can't believe you're still single. Here are some examples … Female comedian: *So, I was bleaching my moustache and crying last night, then I remembered I had half an Easter egg under my bed, and I decided not to kill myself after all. Can you believe I'm still single?*

Male comedian: *So, I've watched so much porn in hotel rooms around the English-speaking world, I once went three days without seeing a human face – just genitals 24/7! I don't know why I'm still single.*

I could tell you lots of reasons why I'm single in a funny way, but I want to tell you the truth. Look at me. No, really, let me tilt your chin up and stare into your eyes. Stop squirming, I won't let you wriggle away until you've 'heard my truth'. Here it is. I am single because, as a robot, I have no heart and am incapable of love. Psyche! I am a regular human girl and I know that I will eventually require some form of lifetime-buddy system.

When there's a man in my life, I've always struggled with what to refer to him as. Even 'the man in my life' sounds stupid, I think. There's plenty of men in my life – my previous dentist was male, my brother is male, the list just goes on and on … I don't like the term 'partner', because it sounds like a business merger. 'The One' leaves me cold. Which One? One of those Ones? That One? Like all immature adults, I find the term 'lover' too hilarious to use. To say I'm 'seeing someone' makes it seem like a waking dream. Can anybody else see this guy? I'm definitely seeing someone – he's right over there, in the rocking chair. Even the classic 'boyfriend' sounds a little adolescent. And I recently discovered that 'my old man' actually means my father.

The propinquity effect often leads us to hook up with someone who's knocking around our locality. I think about how my parents met – they grew up four miles away from each other. Also, they look chillingly alike. I have said too much.

Anyway, I have analysed my routines, and here are the men I see regularly each week. There are three of them:

My best friend, Ian. He is the best, but he is like a sister to me. So it would be weird to choose him romantically over my other sisters, especially considering how much prettier than him they all are. No offence to him.

My trainer, Seán. He is also the best but, technically, I do pay him to spend time with me. I don't think that's a healthy foundation for a romantic relationship. We've all seen *Pretty Woman*.

My neighbour (I don't know his name). He wears a flat cap, not in a hipster way. He has a scraggly dog that barks at other dogs. Often tells the dog to *quiet the fuck down*, in a good-humoured way – the dog ignores him. He looks about sixty, and after living on the same street as me for almost four years, he's only just begun returning my hellos. We may run out of time.

Actually, there's a possible fourth candidate that you should know about. The handsomest man in Ireland works in a café by my old office. The management put him behind the coffee bar by the window: a highly visible spot – they're no fools. Me and every other woman meanders by his spot real slow, taking it all in. He's always up to something. One day he's concentrating on a latte; the next he is polishing glasses. You just never know with him. Looking in the window to catch a glimpse of him became such a part of my daily routine that once I accidentally waved at him. He looked sort of hunted but did wave back, in a noncommittal way. I like him because he's handsome, punctual and has a cool bike. However, he does look kind of mournful and self-involved. I used to be into that but now, not so much. He's going to lose me if he's not careful.

I guess, for now, I'm a player, and you know what that means. I'll just keep playin'. *The game is all I know – don't take it personally, Babe. See? I can't even remember your name, that's how irresistible a mix of haughty and insecure I am!*

If I do decide to get married to this barista, one thing is certain. I am absolutely *not* having a hen weekend. He can have a stag party if he wants (I get the feeling that he wouldn't; however, as I have yet to speak to him, I can't be 100 per cent certain), but there's no chance you'll find me wearing a garter and an L-plate, surrounded by reluctant acquaintances who have been invited on the grounds that they are hard drinkers and female.

I get nervous when men and women are segregated. It has historically scary undertones and nowadays only happens in terrible places, like prison, or on the game show *Take Me Out*. When my friend Cassie got engaged, she swore she would have nothing like a conventional wedding. Her exact words were: *No bloody priest, no shitty kitchen party and absolutely no fucking hen!* As night follows day, she folded. Before I knew it, I found myself sitting on the train to Kilkenny with a bottle of WKD in my hand. I joined the hen party for the second night only, which is just about acceptable, socially.

I should have come clean and said it wasn't my thing. I should have been honest and just taken Cassie out to lunch another time, but I went along obediently. I went out of a sense of duty and a loyalty to tradition that I feel when it comes to my oldest friends. I think it must be similar to how liberal-minded British people feel about the royal family. They strike out alone, and complain about how unchanging and constricting the Windsors are, then a big public occasion comes along and they find themselves cutting the crusts off sandwiches and welling up when they hear the national anthem.

Even girls who were mean to me in school still have some kind of wicked hold on me. I watch myself around those ones, amazed at how quickly I revert to being a cowed teenager. The last hen party I had been on with them was four years previously, in Lisbon. We arrived in the middle of a city-wide sardine festival. Strung all around, there were washing lines of sardines, in various stages of desiccation. Lisbon, from what I could glimpse behind the rows of silvery fish, was pretty and hilly. I didn't care, because I was terrified.

I'm afraid of fish, see? I fainted the last time I went to an aquarium. I can't bear to look at them and dread the idea of touching them. You know how, when you're a small child, you can scare yourself rigid by pretending there's a clown or a paedophile under the bed? Well, I can achieve the same terrified ecstasy tonight, simply by getting under the covers and imagining that if I move my toe even an inch to the right, it will brush off a carp.

Now, allow me to lie on your couch and tell you where I think it all began. As you know, I'm from Cobh, which is an island. Fish were my neighbours for a long time, and I wasn't always scared of them. I used to pick them up and everything. Sometime around September, mackerel lose their tiny minds and fling themselves onto the strand. You don't even have to fish for them – you just saunter around and collect them. They jump out of the water because they want to have sex real bad. They want to dance with somebody; they want to feel the HEAT with somebody. With somebody who loves them. I was more than happy, back then, to fill buckets full of struggling fish. But all of that changed when my brother arrived home one day with a particularly athletic goldfish.

This guy could travel great distances, and jump and soar – right out of his tank and across the floor. We had to get a special lid for him. It was my turn to clean the tank one Saturday morning and the second I removed the lid, he sailed across the room and slam-dunked himself into the wastepaper basket. He rustled around in the papers and sweet wrappers, and I searched and searched but couldn't find him. I tipped the bin out and he flipped across the floor and under the bed. He just kept running away from me. It freaked me out so badly that I hid in the wardrobe and called my mother. She was playing her Paul Robeson record super-loud in the kitchen, so didn't hear me. After about six minutes, the fish hurled himself against the wardrobe door and I had to come out. He glared at me and I shakily put him back in his tank. Ever since then, I've been scared of him and all his cousins.

That's one of the reasons why I wasn't excited to be on a hen weekend in Lisbon during the goddamn *Festas da Cidade*. Although even the scariest sardines were not as threatening as some of the girls on the hen. I still think about this one incident that played out in the hotel room when we were getting ready to go out. One girl said: *I know it's bad, but I had to take a photo of this heifer on the beach today – look at the size of her and she's in a BIKINI!* She passed the phone around. There was a lady in a navy-blue bikini with a shiny black ponytail, standing on the sand, one hand on her hip, talking to a little boy – he was smiling and holding a rag. I think it was one of those comfort blankets, or the remnants of one. Most of the girls weren't too responsive. Margo said: *Jesus wept* – but she says that about everything. Sharon was the angriest. She studied the photo for ages, and said: *And she's absolutely delighted with herself – fucking GROSS!* Then she went back to sucking in her face, to better dust the jutting-out parts with bronzing powder.

Of course, there was nothing gross about the photo except the photographer. That's a good line, and one that I failed to say on the day. To register my disapproval, I chose the old chestnut of just going quiet for a moment. Remaining silent was as brave a statement as I could muster. Bam! A regular Joan of Arc, that's me.

So, that was Lisbon. You'd have a better time there, I'm sure. Go! Go and sit in the large, cold halls they have there, tiled in blue and white and staffed by short men in dicky bows serving custard tarts and custard tarts alone. The minimum order is a half dozen, honestly, and they arrive at your table warm and dusted with cinnamon. Knock yourself out. As long as you're not afraid of fish and you actually like your friends, you'll have a ball.

Now we were all set for a new adventure in Kilkenny. What better way to kick off the afternoon than attending a cocktail-making lesson? Alternative activities mentioned during the organising stages were salsa dancing or having spa treatments. Of all the activities in the world, those were our options, lined up in a series of e-mails that got more passive-aggressive as the weekend neared.

> Hi Hens!
>
> Only a month away, so we need to decide on cocktails/salsa/facials – let me know your pref by 5 p.m. today. Can't wait! We must have a great wkend for Cass, it's about her not us, so I know you're all busy but get back to me ASAP!!
>
> Xxxxx Chief BM

This was followed a day later by:

OK, Chickies, those of you who haven't transferred into my bank account, you HAVE to give me the money for the hotel the minute you arrive – so there's no confusion.

Xxxxx Chief BM

My 'pref' was facials, because I wanted to say to the beauty therapist, as a little joke at the end: *I'm not paying you for the treatment, I'm paying you to leave.* I love getting massages, but I find it hard to relax during them because of this recurring thought I have. I worry that because I have no skills or qualification, I may very well end up becoming a television presenter. It wouldn't be the worst thing in the world, unless I end up becoming one who gets a massage on TV all the time. Of all the tragic jobs available in television today, I will be very disappointed if I have to wrap up an item on a studio-based daytime TV show by fake-shooing away the camera saying: *Now, off you go – I'm trying to relax!* I will know then that I failed to make the most of my one go-round on this earth. My disappointment won't show, because there will more than likely be a producer there, forcing me to 'keep it showbiz'. So I'll smile blissfully, cover my deadened eyes with cucumber slices and sigh, as the camera pans away.

So I wasn't too cut up about it when the rest of the women on the hen chose cocktail lessons over the spa. There are lots of things that annoy me about spas (said the Little Duchess, tapping her plump fingertips together). I don't like candles lighting in the daytime. I don't like lying on a wooden deckchair indoors. I don't like being in a dressing gown and reading about celebrities. I don't find it relaxing when a lady breathes into my ear: *You have lovely skin*. I can only truly relax by listening to a radio documentary and chewing on a plaque-disclosing tablet, then brushing my teeth until I draw blood. I guess I'm just a very sensuous woman.

I was also glad to avoid salsa lessons, as I hate anything foreign. Just clowning, dog! Sure aren't I forever in the ethnic food aisle of my local Dunnes Stores, buying up the enchilada kits? Truthfully, I'm too clumsy for any type of dance that is not highly individualistic. I bop my knees off things and regularly bang my head. I often have the type of bruises Radiohead sing about: ominous ones, that don't heal. I currently have an intense bruise striped right across my thigh, which looks thrillingly like a sexy-time injury. It actually happened when I fell over my bike, trying to get to my sister's phone to read her new text message before she got to it. It wasn't immediately painful – before it hit me, I had time to shout: *I bet it's only Mammy anyway*. Like many middle-class dopes, I think black eyes and scars and serious bruises are kind of impressive. I want to show loads of people my bruise, but in order to do so, I have to pull my jeans down. Apparently that is not cool – at least according to the tram inspector. I'll tell him what's not cool: being an uptight frigid old relic, that's what! Get a real job, on an actual train, why don't you?

Are you embarrassed for me because I call my mother 'Mammy'? I know it sounds babyish. But I don't think I can switch to calling her by her actual name, just because I'm thirty. So I remain, like a modern-day Shirley Temple, stuck with a little-girl voice and ringlets, bleating at my sister for all eternity: *I bet it's only Mammy anyway*.

Back to the cocktail-making, which took place in a large conference room on the top floor of a four-star hotel. I suppose that's all the room is being used for during the recession, because business people don't have anything to meet up and chat about. Two paper plates of Doritos, thirty women and six bottles of vodka. The surly barman did a head count and said that there were four people missing, so we'd have to make up the price. It was an extra €1.80 each, and he said he required payment before the lesson commenced. There was much searching through clutch bags, looking for change. Then the chief bridesmaid said that the bride shouldn't have to pay. The barman recalculated, and it was more like €2.15 each, so more searching and coin-counting ensued. It sure was an awkward start to an already uncomfortable gathering. Hen parties are tricky social events, because they consist of a group of people with not enough in common thrown together for too long. Often all they share with each other is a hatred of drinking through penis-shaped straws and a connection to the bride to be, who's too busy looking after her hammered future mother-in-law to actually talk to any of them.

OK, first up we have 'Sex on the Beach' or 'Sand in your Bottom', as some people call it.

With that happy sentiment muttered by the already bored barman, we were off! There was a workman at the far end of the room for the entire duration of the lesson, tinkering with sockets. I found him unconvincing and assumed he was the stripper. Nobody acknowledged his presence, so that confirmed it for me. The chief bridesmaid went around to us all individually and whispered that we had to *get Cassie absolutely locked before the stripper, and I mean plastered.*

I looked over at the stripper: he was doing some grouting and had quite a lot of emulsion in his hair and eyebrows. I asked the chief bridesmaid when he was going to start dancing. I had to point him out three times before she saw him – the man wearing the high-visibility vest, inside the conference room, puttying away onto the wall. She told me that he wasn't the stripper, that she didn't know who he was, and that we would have to move on to a pub by 8 p.m., to await our sweet Prince there. I realised then that the schedule left no room for dinner. I ran to my room and ordered room service. Beef. I would need my strength.

Don't get me wrong, there were some great ladies there too, of course. Early on, I even met a new girl. An unexpected ally! I knew as soon as I set eyes on her, and she said she liked my nails. I had painted them a flesh colour that made it look like I had never-ending fingers – extremely unflattering but very alluring, I thought. And so did she! She had worked with Cassie in Ben & Jerry's one summer, where she ran the flavour graveyard – she decided which flavours to resurrect. Also, she self-identified as a feminist. Dream lady! Be my friend? And she was, briefly.

Unfortunately for our burgeoning relationship, she decided to deal with the whole hen party business by drinking herself into a state that made it all seem faraway and therefore more tolerable. We said our goodbyes, as she drifted off. Physically, she remained close by, but after the first hour of hard liquor, she was not really there anymore. The last I saw of her, she was carrying out her dare, which was to fake an orgasm in the middle of the pub. I didn't blame her for leaving me. At a hen party, it's every man for himself. My own coping mechanism involved nipping out to phone one sister every hour, and furtively eating peanut M&Ms from my handbag.

The first clue that the stripper was on his way was that the barman in the pub started to cover all the smoke alarms with latex gloves. I asked him what he was doing, and he said that he had to cover them – that if he didn't, then the stripper's smoke machine would set them off. The fact that we were upstairs in a pokey old bar with no working smoke alarms made me feel anxious, until a thought struck me and I was calm again … A fire, although terrible, would surely end the night.

There had been excitement among the girls when the chief bridesmaid said the stripper sounded foreign on the phone. The general consensus was that a Polish stripper would be ideal, because they work out. Even Sharon – who had earlier refused to get into a taxi because a black man was driving it – agreed with that. I started to make a list of races that were acceptable to her, in order to trace her logic later.

The music suddenly ramped up and a short, stocky fireman raced up the steps. For a second I panicked, and regretted wishing for a fire – but I quickly realised this wasn't a real fireman, because he had no vest on. I thought the stripper would do a dance, and then slowly strip off. I was kind of imagining that type of dance you do when you're messing around and drying yourself off after a swim in the sea. But it was nothing like that. He didn't dance, or do an ironic striptease: he just quickly yanked off his plastic fireman's jacket, whipped down his tracksuit bottoms and stood before us in white sports socks, white runners and a peach-coloured thong. It was confronting, let me tell you.

He wasn't in great shape, physically. This offended some of the girls, who, in thirty seconds, went from screaming with excitement to yelling things like *Gross!* and *He's disgusting!* and *He's not even Polish!* I don't know where he was from, but he looked South American and had a Spanish accent. He really horrified Sharon who, as she took a photo, called out: *Yock, you look like a fucking monkey.*

The whole thing lasted about four minutes. It was especially centred on Cassie. He hauled her up on a barstool and, basically, mounted her. The girls circled around, screaming again. Cassie looked unhappy but managed a few smiles and waves from behind his thrusting bottom. As it continued, she began pushing him away, saying things like *No, no* and *Please stop!* I thought I saw tears in her eyes, but everyone was laughing and filming it on their phones, so we were actually having a great time – right? I had a sudden urge to phone the police. I talked myself down. Could I actually turn myself in for paying a stranger to assault my friend? I sat there, struck dumb once again.

It ended quite suddenly. The volume of the music was lowered and the stripper asked if anyone else wanted to dance or feel his quads. The girls shoved one of the older ladies towards him and he ground into her for a moment, but everyone quickly lost interest. He got back into his plastic fireman's uniform and sprinted away, clutching his €300. I checked the time. It was only 9.30 p.m.

Imagine what is happening where you are not

I'm not a very intrepid traveller. In my chosen profession as an adults' entertainer (always cheeky – never blue), I work exclusively in English-speaking countries. I am anxious about how little of the world I've seen. Globetrotters sense this insecurity, the way a dog senses fear. Or walkies. When I have the misfortune of encountering such people, they take one sniff and proceed to quiz me mercilessly: *So, Maeve, have you travelled much?*

I try and come up with a good answer, but I can't focus. I can't shut out the sound of their ethnic bracelets jangling around and around: *Um, yes, sort of – like, I've been to America.*

Central America?

No, just … normal America. It was good – amazing people, so friendly: it really is the land of smiles.

Oh, right. Did you make it to Alaska? I camped under the Northern Lights in minus twenty degrees: it was incredible, blew my mind to smithereens. Almost lost my fingers.

Then I'll reply: *No, I didn't make it up there, actually. I did go on a really long train trip in New Zealand once, though, and it was so nice. They had this amazing chicken curry in the dining carriage …*

Was it Goan?

What? Where?

I mean the curry – you haven't lived until you've eaten Goan curry. Before I could say I had in fact eaten Goan curry at a music festival once, and therefore have in fact, lived, they'll add: *In Goa.*

These bores (that I'm envious of) can be stopped quickly enough by you holding your finger up to their lips and saying: *You know, I have travelled too. I have travelled all over, my friend … in my mind.*

Then take your finger away and walk out of the room backwards, maintaining eye contact, with your head tilted slightly to one side, for as long as they will allow. This isn't always practical, though – if you're on an aeroplane, for example, or you are related to them. Relations are always popping up at family events, and continuing conversations exactly where they were left off. I still owe one of my uncles an explanation for dropping down to foundation-level Maths in the Leaving Certificate. I successfully distracted him with pavlova the last time we met – at a christening in 1998 – but I know that as soon as he sees me at the next funeral, he'll want the end of my sorry tale.

I don't always run away when someone asks me that competitive question: *So, where have you 'done'?* I stay and fight, because, actually, I have an ace up my sleeve. When they start talking about Song Khran and how Vientiane is the new Barcelona, I bust out my A-game. When pressed, I drop the A-bomb on them. You must have guessed it by now. What place begins with the letter 'A' and is the ultimate travel brag for middle-class Europeans? Not Achill Island, though that is lovely on a misty night. I'm talking about Africa! *Africa!* That's right. I used to live on the Dark Continent. Africa loves that nickname.

We moved to Zimbabwe for a couple of years when I was nine. The story goes that my father was offered a good job there, and he could bring all of us with him – not like his job in England, where he missed his kick-line of chubby toddlers and earnest pre-teens, not to mention his smokin' hot lady. That's the official line, but I don't actually believe we moved there for my father's work. I've long suspected my parents of being undercover scientists conducting a secret, lifelong experiment on us children. Here are some of their theories:

–   We won't allow them to say 'shut up'. However, they may give dead legs.

–   One pair of wellies between two children is more than enough.

–   If a younger one gets chased by a neighbour's dog and an older one doesn't make a sufficient effort to chase that dog in turn, then the older one will get into trouble.

–   We will do everything in our power to convince them that cheese on toast is a treat food.

One day the scientists got bored of us wearing identical duffel coats in the winter and picking gooseberries in the summer, and wondered what would happen if they took all of these children to live in a place that was exactly the opposite of their current environment.

The build-up to our leaving was phenomenal. The school threw us a goodbye party that left both classrooms smelling like salt-and-vinegar crisps for a week. We got inoculated against all sorts of diseases that my brother Oliver knew about from the *National Geographic* magazine. Our grandparents went very quiet. We went to Cork city and got new shoes and dresses in one size too big for the first Christmas we'd spend in Africa. All our aunts, uncles and cousins came to the airport to see us off. We left them waving at us, and headed for the departure gate: an optimistic troop of little bumpkins off on a huge adventure.

None of us children had been on a plane before and I was hyper-aware of a sign I'd seen at the airport saying: *Do Not Tip the Stewardess*. I didn't know that by 'tip', the sign referred to a gratuity. I spent the whole time on the plane shrinking in my aisle seat when the stewardess came near me, and taking the trays of food she offered me very tentatively, avoiding brushing off her fingers.

When I stepped off the plane, onto the tarmac, I took a deep breath and screamed: *I am home. My people, come to me: I am home.* I was slightly embarrassed to be told that the reason it felt so familiar was that we were just on a stopover, in Heathrow airport. Despite what history and any number of crummy comedians would have you believe, Ireland and England aren't really that different. Naturally, the Irish are more soulful and magical and broke than the English – but that's about it.

Before we moved to Zimbabwe, Cobh was my universe. School meant my particular school, food meant my particular food, and even rain meant my particular rain. The night we arrived in Harare, there was an epic electrical storm. We watched, dumbstruck, from our first ever hotel rooms. Forked lightning, massive thunderclaps and falling sheets of glassy rain: it was like the storm in that Celine Dion video, when her boyfriend crashes his motorbike.

Within a week of leaving Cobh, this is what I realised – there are millions of ways of living. Actually, more than millions. I couldn't sleep for the first week because of jet lag and this growing realisation: that there are countless wildly different ways to experience the world. This had simply not occurred to me before. Now, I saw trees that seemed upside-down, with their roots reaching skyward, and was told that they were actually the right way up. Some other revelations included the following: English is just one language; toys can be made out of wire hangers; people are all different colours and shades of those colours; it's possible to actually own a swimming pool; three people can fit on one bike; mothers can go to work; I have an accent; it's not always possible to know the name of every child in your school; you don't have to wear shoes all the time; potatoes are just like other vegetables; tiny animals can kill you stone dead; and water can run out ...

I felt wide open and giddy. All of us children were the same: dazzled by sunshine and jet lag and brand new fruit. Everything was subject to change, even breakfast. My father has only ever cooked two things in his life. Leek and potato soup: once. Porridge: a thousand times. Since the late 1970s, when his children started popping up around the kitchen table, he has made vast pots of pale gloop for us. He soaked the oats at night and everyone else thought it was delicious, but I always hated porridge. I would wake up, furious, to the smell of it. I would then sulk over a bowl of the stuff, having drowned it in milk and drenched it with as much sugar as I could hope to get away with. I swore that when I grew up, I'd always have a revolving selection of sugary cereals to choose from. Real sophisticated, you know? Not like my oafish family, with their poverty gruel.

My dream came true before I had time to grow up. When we first arrived in Zimbabwe, we stayed in a hotel for three weeks, as our house wasn't ready to move into. And you know what hotels have instead of bubbling pots of manky old porridge? They have breakfast buffets, with a *revolving selection of sugary cereals to choose from*. My parents were far too distracted to police what I ate for breakfast. My mother was pregnant and nauseous and my father was working from dawn, so the greediest little girl in the world got her wish! I jumped out of bed in the mornings, then fidgeted and fought with my brother, until I got my hands on a big old bowl and an even bigger spoon and then I would go to claim my prize. It was absolutely wrong of Cecil Rhodes and those other corpulent white men to charge around claiming huge sections of Africa for themselves. I can understand why they did it, though. I can confirm that it is a place full of strange, beautiful birds, glittering caves of precious minerals and boxes and boxes of those little devils called Corn Puffs, with their big yellow taste and sweet puffed crunch.

Back to the house party: back to the queue for the bathroom with no paper, and back to the persistent questions from a man in fisherman's pants about how much of the world I have successfully 'done'. Back to the sweet smell of the ganja in Rathmines, am I right? *Holla!* I boasted for quite a while: about snakes in my shoes, about learning local songs and eating sadza with one hand. Then I got overtaken by gloom, thinking about the state poor, great Zimbabwe is in today. So I said goodbye to Old I've-Been-All-Over-Le-Roux and headed home. It was late but I couldn't sleep.

It's hard to know what to do when you can't sleep and nobody else is up. Some people sip hot milk with honey while watching death porn. Me, I pop off a couple of magnesium tablets and set my brain to *Imagine What Is Happening Where You Are Not*. This is a method of drifting off that I invented when we moved to Zimbabwe and I figured out that there is a lot going on in the world that I don't know about. The method is as follows: as you lie in bed, simply picture what everyone else is up to. You may come up with something new, or use people you've seen and places you've been – or cobble together a combination of the two.

That night I thought about a waiter in Geneva whisking an egg into the remains of a pot of cheese fondue, as a table of people applauded him. I imagined an old lady in giant sunglasses on the Upper West Side of Manhattan, walking a small white dog. I saw a woman, with no bra on, strutting past a dumpling stall in London, and a zookeeper in Berlin feeding mackerel to a moody polar bear. A nun missed a bus in Accra, while in Beijing, a boy's heart leapt when he heard the beep of a text message. A grandfather thought for a while, then ordered a slice of banana bread in an Auckland café, and another small girl in Harare began to figure out that she wasn't the centre of the universe after all.

Mergers and acquisitions

I've learned all I know about the business world from the Melanie Griffith film *Working Girl*. In it, she plays a softly spoken secretary who's always coming up with great ideas for business deals, but keeps getting shafted by her bosses. In the end, it works out great for her – she cuts her hair, dumps her boyfriend and gets a job in a corporation as an executive in 'mergers and acquisitions', with a corner office of her own. Hurrah! She also sleeps with Harrison Ford, proving that we *can* have it all. Gratuitous shots of her in her underwear aside, it's a great film.

My favourite scene in *Working Girl* – apart from the bit where Harrison Ford takes off his shirt – is a business meeting scene. It takes place on the top floor of a skyscraper in a dark-panelled boardroom, with men in suits and documents and coffee. I love the scene because it makes me nostalgic for my childhood.

Just before I turned seven, my mother began to call bi-monthly meetings around our kitchen table. The time, location and minutes of each meeting were recorded by our father in a large maroon book. The purpose of these meetings was to ensure we all had a chance to say what was on our minds, and that nobody would get lost in the gang. We would air our grievances and record our achievements. Even the baby of the family was included, as evidenced in the following extract from the Book of Minutes.

You will need to know some key characters. Geraldine was a goat; Christmas was a cat; and Binky was a car. This was the final meeting held before we moved to Zimbabwe for two years. We children ranged in age from two to twelve.

Sunday, 17 September 1989

Dear old Geraldine died of old age and Christmas died on the road, so we said a little prayer.

Daddy: Congratulations to Raedi, for settling into school.

Raedi: When we come back from Africa, we can get another goat.

Ettie: I hope Mammy doesn't have any more headaches.

Mammy: Any children visiting her should not go upstairs.

Lilly: Just say to them: 'Play with the other girls awhile, while I go upstairs to get something.'

Oliver: Too much milk is being spilled – use a jug.

Mammy: We hope Daddy and the lads had a good time at the christening.

Rosey: Congratulations to Daddy, on getting the new shoes for me and the lads! (IR£164 in Crofts yesterday.)

Lilly: We all pulled together last week, when Daddy was in England.

Ettie: Raedi should have a hanky going to bed.

Lilly: The chicks under the stairs woke me this morning.

Rosey: I love pavlova.

Maeve: We had a brilliant week, even without Daddy.

Mammy: The lads should keep their school clothes separate, to cut down on washing. Change into your old clothes as soon as you come home from school. Those old clothes should last about a week.

Lilly: If we offer Rosey something, she says no, but if Mammy offers her something, she says yes.

Rosey: I'd like to buy a book like that. (A pop-up book.)

Ettie: I'm really looking forward to buying a new doll in Midleton Craft Show next week. Daddy, your new tooth is lovely.

Daddy: Congratulations to Mammy, for nursing the crow back to good health during the week!

Oliver: Well done, for carrying the crow to freedom down in the bog and for getting pecked.

Mammy: If you're at a party like Maeve was yesterday, you don't have to stay if you don't want to. Phone or walk home.

Rosey: I like the horsies.

Raedi: Congratulations to Daddy, for going back to England and for tidying the whole place up!

Daddy: Raedi, it's your job to mind the chickies. Lilly – water the blackcurrant bushes.

Everyone wished Cork the best of luck in the All-Ireland Final.

We all said we were sad to sell Binky but she will be done up by her new owner. The meeting then ended, at 2.45 p.m.

When I read over the Meeting Book, I feel all sorts of things. I feel incredibly lucky to be part of a gang that grew up in an Enid Blyton/Alice Taylor pop-up book of our own, without any scary parts. I love that my parents valued our opinions enough to listen to and record them so carefully – even more so now that I understand how busy and broke and young they were back then. I remember why I hate parties. I marvel at the convenience of both Geraldine and Christmas shuffling off this mortal coil just before we moved to another continent – and wonder why we didn't have our customary pet burial for them.

Now, you might imagine that, with such a high-powered history of business meetings behind me, I'd be an expert in the world of business meetings today, but I'm not. It's just that meetings are confusing to me. They should be straightforward, when you think about it: a meeting is just like catching up with a friend, except, instead of talking about your feelings or who you suspect is pregnant, you talk about business. And instead of being a friend, the person is a stranger who wants to make money off you. It's so simple!

Yet I find it hard to be a business version of myself during meetings. I'll take it too far and often hear myself saying things I didn't even know I thought. Once I actually said: *Are you kidding me? I drink five cups of coffee a day!* It is thought to be impossible to truly surprise yourself – that deep down, we all know what we're likely to say and do – but that day I was shocked to discover that I am, in fact, a total asshole.

First of all, I never use the word 'kidding' – it's far from kidding that I was reared. People don't 'kid' each other in Ireland. I'm a country girl: kids to me are baby goats. Also, it's a complete falsehood for me to say I drink five cups of coffee a day: an out-and-out lie. Coffee gives me heart palpitations. I don't know if you've ever had heart palpitations – how could I know that about you? If you haven't, here's what they feel like … You're walking the way you walk, talking the way you talk, smiling the way you smile, then *FLUTTER! CREAK! POP!* goes your heart. It drops and rumbles for a split second, then gets back to business. It's a jolting reminder that when it comes down to it – which it always does – we are powered by one small muscle with its own ideas on how we should behave. It is annoying to realise we are not immortal machines that can do whatever we like and not face any consequences, but as they say in Spain: *c'est la vie*. So I avoid coffee – even though I love coffee. Do you understand? By that I don't mean, *coffee is nice – yum, yum.* No. I *love* coffee. I am *in love* with coffee. This love runs deep. Coffee is my dark mistress, who does not love me back. Coffee is who I think about as soon as I open my eyes in the morning. I want to be the umbrella Coffee remembers to bring with her on a rainy day, the lamp she reads by, the light on her bicycle which keeps her safe. Like a lonely dog, I sniff the air that Coffee has passed through, and long for her.

With that troubled history, I still blithely came out with the *five cups a day* line! I think I said it because there was an American lady at the meeting too, and I'm always showing off in front of Americans. I comfort myself now with the fact that at least I said *coffee*, as opposed to *java* or *black medicine*. Small mercies.

Meetings are difficult to dress for. As you probably know, I own detachable shoulder pads and they come everywhere with me, adding 15 per cent more authority to everything I say while wearing them. So that works out great, but I have a problem with shoes. My problem is when I see a pair, I have to own them! I'm not serious, of course. I hope for your sake you don't know anyone who would actually say that, because – as the character Carrie Bradshaw in *Sex and the City* proved time and again – the more shoes a person has, the more tedious their personality is. My shoe problem is that, not including my flip-flops and furry boots, I only have two pairs, and both of these pairs are white runners. (Don't worry: if I have to go to a wedding, I borrow some shiny, trotter-type things from one of my sisters.) Unless you're an eleven-year-old whizz kid in the computer games industry and everyone wants a piece of you, you probably shouldn't wear runners to a meeting. That's why I always make sure to arrive early for all of my meetings and plant my feet well under a hotel foyer coffee table or a sleeping dog, and then refuse to move until everyone else has left.

It's hard for me to come up with good ideas in meetings, because you don't usually get enough time between thinking something and then saying it. If you want something to be good, filtering time is essential. Proof of that is the first title idea I had for this book when I met with my publisher. How about *Maeve Higgins: Boning My Way to the Top – My Story*, I asked – and she said she'd have to check with her colleagues.

Another time, in a meeting with a producer to come up with potential TV shows, he said to me: *OK! Let's brainstorm!* I had no interest in doing this but didn't want to be rude, so I brightly agreed. We were both quiet for a while, except for him going *do, do, do* and *hmm*, and squinting his eyes a bit. I too made little sounds and pretended to write in my notebook. I really did try to think of ideas, but it was so boring and, because we weren't talking out loud, I got distracted and started to think about other things.

I wondered for a while about this woman I'd been watching earlier that day: she was working in a library in town and had seemed really bored. She was sighing, looking up the catalogue she was reading, and slumping over the counter. I decided that maybe she should have an affair – give herself something to think about other than the Dewey Decimal Classification system. I then spent some time weighing up my options for lunch, and trying to guess how the mackerel I was planning on eating would have stood up to being frozen, then thawed.

Before I could predict what the texture of the fish might be, the producer I was having the meeting with crowded into my view again. *Well?* he says. *What have you got?* I couldn't tell him what I had, so I told him I needed to go to the toilet, urgently. He looked embarrassed for me, but I only said that to buy some time, because a piece of fish and an adulterous librarian does not a hit TV show make.

When I returned, I shoved my feet back under the rug and told the producer I'd had an idea. *Picture this!* I say, in my best pitching voice. *You got a goat and you got a cat. They both go AWOL in rural Ireland – just like that! Vanish into thin air! There's something up. A gang of self-important children, who all look spookily alike, have gotta track 'em down in time to smuggle them to darkest Africa.*

He didn't go for it. Too much of a stretch apparently, nobody would believe it. He said that we should get a java, and try and come up with something else.

Accessible mainstream ideas
for hit TV shows

I was in my room last night, practising some new ways of laughing, when I remembered the meeting with the TV producer and how I couldn't think of any ideas for him. Well, I've thought of some now. And hands off, Aaron Spelling, I've already posted these to myself.

1. Working Title: *Good Dog, Resentful Dog?*

   In this show, we somehow get into the minds of our pets and find out what they really think of us – a truly shocking reality show. I would present it and mediate between pets and owners, after such explosive revelations as: *I actually don't enjoy when you put a beret on me, then hold a saxophone close to my mouth and send photos around to your friends with the caption: 'I'm the Clarence Clemons to your Bruce Springsteen'.*

2. Working Title: *Mr Tetsugoro and the Hurley*

   In this documentary series, I would disguise myself as all sorts of non-Irish nationals – for example,

I would dress up like a Hawaiian teenager or an old Swedish lady. As that character, I would then try out a number of traditionally Irish activities, like road bowling and binge drinking. This should qualify for funding on the grounds of diversity and also as sports and arts broadcasting. Advertisers will flock to it, as it will be popular with the lucrative eighteen to thirty-year-old male audience.

3. Working Title: *Penny For 'em – Maeve asks Michael what he's Thinking.*

A sixty-part series, in which I interview Michael Fassbender about his childhood memories, his hopes for the future, his favourite things about me and all the other stuff that people in love talk about. Michael's involvement has yet to be confirmed, but I can say at this point that he's totally into the idea.

4. Working Title: *Now This is Gold!*

Brick wall … spotlight … microphone … me in a boxy pant suit. A classic stand-up-on-TV show! Those shows always work, right? Wrong, they never do. However, they do get made, and that's what counts. In this series, instead of performing my own stand-up, I would do jokes recommended to me over the years by various people. Examples include:

– Laptop repair man (right after reciting a long tract of a Lee Evans routine about getting a haircut): *So you should do that, absolutely hilarious.* (I checked with him that he meant do the exact same routine and he said yes, and reiterated how funny he found it.)

— Ticket collector on Tralee train: *Light bulbs, right? Sure, they're not that light – some of them are heavy. Well, no, they're light but the thing is, you could do a load of jokes about words like that, that say one thing but they mean the opposite.*

— Kasim (a colleague in the clothes shop where I used to work): *I know what you do jokes about – about a Libyan guy living in Dublin, no? And everything that he is doing, and the pints and all that, no?*

Gibbons swung, birds sang and peacocks peacocked past

The train from Cobh to Cork stops at Fota Wildlife Park. You'll know the stop because somebody has thoughtfully painted the railings around the station house a leopard-print pattern. You'll also know it because the announcer sometimes says: *Alight here please, animals, off you get now* – even if it's a Sunday evening and there are no children on board.

When we were children, my parents often took us to Fota Gardens on weekends. I didn't realise there was a separate wildlife park until I was about eight years old. In a genius move by our broke parents, they tricked us into believing that going to Fota meant going to wander around a garden behind large, ponderous groups of senior citizens.

When I was in first class in school, an announcement was made that Fota was to be our school tour destination. I was slightly disappointed, because I was a regular there. I cheered up when I thought about how I could show everybody the secret paths to the pond and the best elms for climbing. I was also pleased because, no matter what the venue, a school tour always involved my sweet friends and my salty friends: Fanta on the bus, and chips when we got there. I couldn't figure out why everyone in school was so excited about going to see the animals. The only animals I had seen in Fota were a couple of brown guinea hens scratching around the ground and a small pet cemetery beside the house.

Half of our school – about thirty children – got the train for six minutes and disembarked at an entrance to a Fota I had never seen. We went through some turnstiles into a parallel universe. Gibbons swung, birds sang and peacocks peacocked past. Having spent the previous fortnight showing off about how I knew the place like the back of my hand, and insisting that everyone should stick with me and I'd show them the world, I kept very quiet. Looking back now at all those Sunday afternoons in the gardens, I find it hard to believe that I never enquired as to where the screaming monkey noises were coming from. I suppose I was just so engrossed in feeding the ducks that I never thought to ask. When I get that same train today with a crowd of excited children and they begin clamouring to get off at Fota, I always whisper to them that they should make sure and see the giraffes. Creepy, yes, but also helpful.

Since moving to Dublin, I've moved on to bigger train journeys. It really is all go-go-go when you're an important businesswoman like me. I get the train all over the country, except for the whole west of the country, which is not served by rail. A while ago, Irish Rail added a facility whereby you can book your seat online and they put your name on a tiny screen over your seat. In a country the size of Ireland, this is problematic. By our nature, we are curious about each other – bordering on nosy. More than once, I've been stalled in the aisle as some old lady peers at the name over a seat and then at the person sitting in it, saying: *You don't look like the O'Riordans at all – which one of the boys is your father, tell me?* There's a build-up of passengers as connections are made and family trees traced right back.

I don't think it's a great idea to have names over seats. It gives predators and sociopaths an important piece of your jigsaw. You know how they use your name a lot when they talk to you, in the belief that by doing so, you will warm to them? It works on me. Add to that all the other information you give away about yourself on a train journey, and you could be in real trouble. When someone, anyone, says: *And how are you Maeve? You enjoy tea, don't you, Maeve, and you love listening to the radio on your phone, Maeve – give me a fiver, Maeve* – I feel all warm and stoned: they clearly care about me! Before I know it, I do whatever they say. Luckily, I've discovered a way of reserving a seat without giving those monsters any information. I will share that way with you now – prepare yourself!

Here goes … You can put any name you like on the screen – it doesn't have to match the name on your credit card! That discovery allowed me to have a lot of fun when I went on tour around the country in 2011. I went to Westport as Lisa 'Left Eye' Lopes. The 'Don't Go Chasing Waterfalls' singer lived again on that four-hour trip across our narrow little country; she even had a muffin from the trolley as a special treat. Another time, ?uestlove sat happily gazing out the window in a purple dress, drumming his fingers on the table, on his way to Nenagh for the evening. I had to stop assuming the identities of hip-hop legends after my accountant asked me who Mos Def was, and why I was buying him an adult single to Tralee. I sent my accountant a copy of *Black on Both Sides*. That didn't help: turns out he's a West Coast hip-hop purist and I can't claim expenses unless I'm the one travelling.

My ideal train journey involves two key components. One is a good magazine. I read books on trains too, but magazines are better because you can take breaks. If a book is really good, I forget to blink. I gobble it up with my greedy eyes and they get really sore. A magazine can never be that engrossing, so when I have hours to fill, I mix it up a little – a dollop of Dostoyevsky here, a smidgen of Suri Cruise's new hairstyle there. Actually, I haven't read any Dostoyevsky in a long time, not since I was eleven. That's right, haters, I was an unbearable child. I am pleased to say I haven't read any celebrity magazines in a long time either. I can't bear those magazines, but that didn't stop me scarfing them down in waiting rooms and taking guilty gulps of them in newsagents. I had to make a really big effort to stop looking at them. It was hard, because they are so colourful and simple and gossipy, but I feel better for it. Now, for better or worse, I stick to *National Geographic*. It's colourful and simple too, but full of rational thought and actual facts.

I really like *O Magazine* too. Actually, I love *O Magazine*. In case you don't know it – like, if you've been in a coma or are among the three billion people in the world living on less than $2.50 a day – *O Magazine* is Oprah Winfrey's lifestyle magazine! In a stroke of magnificently egocentric genius, she graces the front cover of every copy of every issue, every month. This has been going on for a long time, and even she looks a bit fed up on the past two years' worth of covers. She's smiling and wearing bright citrus colours as always, but there's a faraway look in her eyes. There's a feature on the Oprah website called 'O-Mag YourSELF', which allows you to photoshop your head onto Oprah's body on a selection of covers. I chose the one with her peeking out of a wardrobe. Because I am white, and Oprah's neck and hands are black, the final image is a little jarring, but it's on my wall anyway.

I like the magazine because it has empowering pieces of writing from brilliant people like Maya Angelou, and also funny American recipes for dishes like yam and marshmallow casserole. It teaches me that to Live my Best Life™, all I need to do is a) walk like I've got diamonds between my thighs, and b) put more sugar in my dinner.

The other vital component in a happy train journey is, naturally, the correct outfit. You must wear something loose and comfortable. Your shoes should come off easily. Basically, you should try to dress like you are a resident in a nursing home. My train outfits are exceptional in both their understated old-lady elegance and also in that I am not usually one to wear different things for different activities.

In fact, my current favourite thing about being single is that I can wear something comfortable to bed, then get up, stay wearing it, and sail right on throughout my day. My days are all different – I would tell you what a typical day is, but there's no such thing in my topsy-turvy world. I'm such fun – just you try pinning me down. Good luck! On any given day, I could be getting up to anything – from the washing up, to checking to see if anybody has retweeted me, to sitting on my bed looking at the ground. Who knows? What's important is, if I've slept alone, nobody will notice I never got dressed. Part of me wonders if I will continue to sleep alone, forever, unless I start changing my clothes more regularly. I doubt it. Guys can't get enough of the Higg-bomb, even in the same (extremely comfortable) outfit, 24/7/365.

My sister Ettie thinks that staying in your sleepwear past 7 a.m. is a sign of great degradation and possibly mental illness. She looks concerned, and asks how I am feeling when I wander into the kitchen in my floral pyjama bottoms and my yellow T-shirt saying, *No Shame In My Game*.

Great! I say.

Ettie slips into older sister mode. *Well, you look wrecked. Are you going to have a shower?* I say I'm only doing some writing so there's no real need to be clean, per se. Her humanitarian training and years of dealing with people in crisis kick in at that point, and she says loudly and slowly: *Do you need some help?*

My father has clothes for work, clothes for cycling, clothes for going to the shops in, clothes for barbecuing in. He even has a specific outfit for tipping. 'Tipping' is the preserve of men with farming in their blood, who are now confined to less than an acre. They tip around the place, cutting firewood, clearing out gutters, drowning cats – you know, little, outdoorsy jobs. My father's tipping outfit is an all-in-one suit, in a bright royal blue, with kneepads. It makes him look quite stocky, but he doesn't care about that kind of thing. *I'm going tipping*, he tells my mother and pulls on his tipping suit. My parents really know how to communicate. All they do is keep each other informed about what they're up to, even when they're in clear sight of each other. *I'll put on the kettle*, says my mother, and puts the kettle on, three metres away from my father. *I'll set this fire for the morning*, he

49

explains to her, setting the fire next to where she is sitting, watching him set the fire.

When my father can't see my mother the instant he walks into the house, his plaintive refrain has been the same since I was a child. He looks around and asks, *Where's Mon?* He calls my mother Mon, because that's short for Monica, not because she is a Rastafarian. When I was a teenager I used to say smart-alec things like, *Mon is gone to heaven – we all miss her but it's been thirty years, don't you remember?* But even that didn't stop him – plus it made me feel like I'd be in real trouble if she actually was dead but we didn't know yet.

One day, exasperation led me to point out to him that there were only three places she could be in the house if she wasn't in the kitchen – namely the bathroom, the sitting room or the bedroom. Actually, permission to boast? *Granted.* Thank you, here goes: we also have a conservatory. However, I knew Mammy wouldn't be out there as, despite costly blinds, it's too cold to sit in during winter, and this particular conversation happened in a November. So, I just listed off the first three places and my father seemed happy with those options and went off exploring. Now he checks those rooms before he asks, *Where's Mon?* But I sometimes catch him mouthing it, even when she's there. Sheer force of habit.

My parents even buy train tickets together. My mother hovers just behind my father, and whispers furious instructions to him. He steps up to the ticket window and repeats her words exactly: *Two returns to Mallow, David* – and the ticket lady looks at him funny.

Let us leave the lovebirds waiting on the platform and hop onto the train to Dublin ourselves. Cork to Dublin takes three hours, and that really is an ideal length of time. A lot can be achieved in three hours. As a youngster, Arnold Schwarzenegger famously plotted out his life in five-year increments. I haven't seen his lists, but I'd imagine they go something along the lines of:

1. When I'm done bodybuilding, I'll play the role of a pregnant guy.

2. I'll be in charge of California.

3. I'll make my eyes bulge out to create a distinctive look for myself.

I make my own lists on the train. Some serve solely to wake me up to how limited my ambitions are, like this one:

1. Do a knife skills course.

2. Unfollow ppl on Twitter who talk about telly too much.

3. Find iPod Nano – green bag??

4. Get rid of tracksuit pants, too short.

Other train lists I've made show more cojones. Lately I've been preoccupied with deciding who I want to get rid of in my life and also who I want to see more of. I use train-lists to figure it out. The people I can't get enough of are easy: I just write their names down and plot some way of spending time with them – like this:

1. Anna – go to This Is Knit/coffee.

2. Aoife – lunch (ask her to do that chicken thing).

The other group, the ones I want to cut off, are far trickier. I know the main reason everybody is emigrating at the moment is economic, but I suspect a small percentage of people starting new lives in faraway countries are doing so because it's the only way they can break up with an especially limpet-like friend. It's hard to break up with friends. I feel guilty about it, though I shouldn't, because we all need to at some stage, for whatever reason. In case anyone finds my notebook and sends me to the ning-nong hospital, I write their names in code, for example:

1. Needy.

2. Sexist.

3. No-fun-anymore.

4. Eats-with-her-mouth-open.

5. Touches-me-too-much.

See? You can't tell who I mean. They could just be characters from *Snow White* or maybe a gang of unpopular Native Americans.

It's hard to believe, I know, but I'm sure that even as I write my list, someone underneath this same sky is scheming a way to get rid of me. I hope I'll be gracious about it. I'm on the lookout for signs already. The obvious ones are when someone doesn't reply after you've communicated with them in three different ways. It's possible to miss a text or an e-mail – but a kissogram? Or – when you've arranged to meet them and they don't show up, repeatedly, you must see that they are politely letting you know they don't actually want to meet you. Blanking you on the street is another giveaway. When you've noted these incidents, politely leave the relationship to die. It's for the best.

On trains, I also make lists of which recipes and ingredients I want to try out – but I won't bore you with that. Let's just say that as we (mercifully) whizzed past Thurles one evening, I suddenly remembered reading a cool recipe for salt-baked celeriac, and the following day I made it.

Another great way to pass the time is to just look out the window. Train windows are like cinema screens, or those TVs everyone got during the Celtic You-Know-What. They are so big, and the speed with which things pass is almost hypnotic. You can get some quality daydreaming time in. If it's a quiet journey, your mind can cover all sorts of terrain, from Right Said Fred lyrics to the fact that nothing lasts forever.

However, you can't stare out the window and daydream when you're faced with an old man all amped up for a mega chat-party. That's what happened to me the last time I went to Galway. It was tough because this particular fellow's choice of topics left me with nowhere to go. First he asked me about GAA, of which I know very little. I said to him vaguely: *Oh yes, aren't Cork good?* He laughed loudly and for ages.

I then said something I'd heard on the radio: *They're a young team* – thus exhausting my knowledge of the topic. The old man agreed and spoke at length about the ages of other teams, and also the rules of the game and the tournaments coming up. I'm ashamed of myself for not caring about hurling and football, and one day I plan to educate myself about them. That afternoon, though, I didn't want to be schooled, so I sneaked a look around to see if there were any free seats. There weren't, so Michael 'Mike D' Diamond had to stay where she was. Without a shred of encouragement from me, Father-Time-Chatterbox-Le-Roux moved on to how stupid politicians are and how all they do is lie and steal from old people. I didn't agree with this so I just said: *Hmm.* That is how you know I disagree with something. I say: *Hmm.* It is passive-aggressive but I prefer to look at it as a charming quirk.

I felt slightly bad for not engaging with Old-Grandad talks-a-lot-Le-Roux in any real way. Sometimes, I am that person who needs to talk. However, I always try and find something my chat victim is actually interested in talking about, and I make sure to give them toilet breaks. I am partial to a friendly rush of chat at the end of the journey. Going through the final tunnel to Kent station in Cork is the ideal time to strike up a conversation: *Were you just up for the day?* A quick exchange comparing the Marks & Spencer in Dublin to the one in Cork, followed by a smiling goodbye does me just fine.

Even with the magazines and the friendliness, there is something about long train journeys that makes me quite melancholy. I don't know if it's the motion, or the introspection, or maybe the way other people look so vulnerable when they're asleep. Maybe it's because on a train you're in between places. For me, it's probably all of those things, as well as a sugar comedown from the hot chocolate

I get at the station. I've found that it's possible to shake off most of the heaviness by plunging into wherever I've ended up, and not thinking too much about the time spent getting there. But no matter how busy I am, there's still a residual touch – a very light one – of sadness after the train.

A large splash of cold, cold cream

When I was thirteen, I had a sleepover in my friend's house and woke up early to find her chubby mother alone in the kitchen. She asked what I'd like for breakfast, and I said Corn Flakes. She kindly busied herself getting a bowl and milk, but began struggling to open a carton of cream with her pudgy little hands. I was starting to find the whole scene dispiriting to watch – but my qualms were forgotten when I tasted her creation: Corn Flakes, milk, a few slices of banana and a large splash of cold, cold cream. It was a proper smashing-in of the door to the Temple of Gluttony, and after that, I never lost the taste for excessive dairy. Particularly cream.

If I had my way, I'd rearrange the food pyramid I learned about in school, to include – and these are scientific measurements – way *less* bread and way *more* cream. (On a side note, I studied Home Economics for six years in school, yet I remain unmarried. Minister for Education, whoever you are – *J'accuse!*)

I like my cream like my men: cold and thick. Just clowning! Well, I'm serious about the cream, and clowning about the men.

56

Do you know Butlers Chocolate Cafés? They are a chain of cafés and, for just thirty cents extra, they put real cream in their drinks. And they also give you a free chocolate with each drink. Though I'd imagine the cost is built into the price of the coffee. (You stick with me – I didn't do Junior Certificate Commerce for no reason!) Anyway, I went through a phase of buying a hot chocolate every Tuesday after my Pilates class. Just in case my core would get too strong and lose the run of itself, I'd make sure to fill it full of dairy and sugar to remind it who's boss. One day my Laser card was rejected by the machine, and I had no cash. I was mortified, and much more embarrassed about running out of money for an expensive chocolate drink than I would have been if I'd have been buying apples or baby clothes or some other worthy thing. The unnecessary luxury of it, my greediness and my stupidity with money – all these combined to make me powerfully ashamed of myself. I turned bright pink and screamed: *I'll be right back with the money!* The man behind the counter was very nice about it, saying, with a warmly Latin wave of his hand: *Take your drink, come back later with the money.*

But I insisted on leaving the hot chocolate there, and that blasted free truffle with it, until I'd borrowed money from my friend Ian, who has an office close by. At times like this, overwhelmed by guilt for such an insignificant reason, I realise how powerful an over-reliance on dairy combined with a Catholic upbringing really is.

The worst thing that's ever happened to me in a restaurant occurred moments after I ordered banoffee pie. Banoffee pie is not so much a dessert, as an assembly of deadly substances. It's a triple dairy threat, with butter in the biscuit base, condensed milk in the caramel layer and cream forming the entire 'lid'. You can bump it up to a quadruple threat, with a sprinkle of chocolate on top if you like. Ask any cardiologist and they'll tell you: it tastes wonderful. Anyway, back to that scene in the restaurant – I was excited when the banoffee arrived and immediately took a big old spoonful, as is my way. Some twerp in the kitchen had put salt instead of sugar into the cream! This real-life nightmare hit me with the first mouthful. Just when I should have been floating away to Happy Land, I got the shock of my life. It was like my favourite poodle snapping at me, or a taxi driver saying something weird about immigrants.

If you ask me – which nobody ever has – whether I think there is any need to put sugar in cream in the first place, I will tell you straight: absolutely not. When you have cream with a sweet thing or a savoury thing, its purpose is to dull everything down into a stoned, dairy haze, not add flavour. And I don't like vanilla in cream. As for Chantilly cream, I'd even go so far as saying that I believe it is the potpourri of dairy. It's dated and try-hard, and I laugh at it.

Something good came of that terrible night in the restaurant, though. I have since developed a special gift. From that day to this, I can tell whether or not milk or cream is on the turn or has been tampered with in some way. One sniff, and I know. I just know! It amazes people and has become something of a party trick of mine. I shouldn't boast, but I actually possess a number of unique skills like that. For example, I can tell my knives just from their handles: I don't have to remove them individually from the knife block, like some dopes do. Also, I can tell if babies are male or female almost all of the time. I mean, just by their faces, even if they have no lipstick on, or visible tattoos. I'd like to put this to the test, fair and square. My dream is to get a hundred babies lined up, dressed in gender-neutral suits, and to be given twenty seconds to shout either *boychild* or *girlchild*. I just don't have that kind of access to babies right now, so you'll have to take my word for it. Actually, if you are Master of any of the major maternity hospitals and you are reading this, please consider letting me into one of those big halls, where you keep the babies like so many rows of adorable potatoes. I will stun you with my incredibly fast and extremely accurate gender pronouncements.

There are four types of people in this world that I don't understand or trust:

- Recreational fisherfolk.

- Supremely confident teenagers.

- Men who are overly tactile, in an entitled sort of way.

- People who forget to eat.

The last lot are the worst. You know, those infuriating ones who say things like: *And then I looked at my watch and it was four o'clock and I STILL hadn't had lunch – didn't even cross my mind!*

You dingbat! You should eat every three hours for your metabolism's sake. Think about your energy levels – up and down and all over the bloody place. If your stomach didn't make contact with your brain to tell you to hurry up and put something in your mouth, then you should be worried, not boastful. You need to wise up, wise guy.

Well, well, mutters my therapist. *Didn't group number four really touch a nerve!?* Whatever, Doctor! I pay you to tell me I'm fine, so quit muttering.

I think about food a lot. Too much, sometimes. On a bad day a packet of digestives is my heaven and hell, rolled up together in a red plastic wrapper and coming in at the princely sum of €1.89. The digestives promise that if I eat them, I can stop worrying about eating them. I tell them they're crazy. I ask them if they seriously believe that they can control me. Depending on how bad the day actually is, they either nod triumphantly or they slink away. When they win, and I eat them, our exchange continues.

Why did you do that? they cry. *Why? You should have let us be!*

I am indignant. *You bloody made me eat you, you little pricks!*

Us? We are just dumb biscuits! We didn't make you do anything. You're out of control!

Maybe I am, but you know how cool guys numb themselves from the pain of being artistic, misunderstood heroes by using speedballs and whiskey? Girls, unsure of where they stand in the world, use sausage sandwiches and almond fingers in a similar way. Sort of a relief valve from thinking all the time. It's far from ideal. When I go to a party and someone asks me: *What's your poison?* I think: *An entire packet of biscuits please – bring butter and tea too, then close the door and let us be.* But I actually say: *Soda and lime, please – and don't worry if you don't have any lime.*

Vocabulary around food is really quite important. If you are fat, it might be helpful to check which words you use around food. If you order anything by the bucket, platter or wheel, you should check yourself before you wreck yourself. I am speaking with the voice of experience. The same voice that once ordered such a large pizza over the phone, it felt the need to fake a pause right after the pizza man said: *If you order one more side, you get a free dessert – would you like to do that?* That pause allowed time for a non-existent consultation with an imaginary dining companion. Then – and bear in mind this is that exact same voice which warns you to watch your words: *Yes, we would. We will take the dough balls with BBQ dip and the strawberry cheesecake ice cream* – then the voice whimpers for a second in an all too familiar and defeated way.

I am old now, though, and wise. I have come up with two great ways of stopping myself from eating buckets, platters and wheels of food that is not good for me. Here they are;

1. Act like you're about to die in a violent or unusual way

This way, the contents of your stomach will eventually be revealed to the general media in a coroner's report. You don't want to be mortified in the afterlife by the existence back on Earth of a printed account of three partially digested jambons, followed by an entire family-sized bag of M&Ms, do you?

2. Ask yourself if you would be happy to eat what you are about to eat in front of Michael Fassbender.

If it's half a lobster fresh from the sea and cooked in butter, and it's lunchtime – fine. *Watch me Michael, learn from me.* If I stop in a garage on the way home from a mediocre show in Waterford and the Cuisine de France pecan plaits are half price because it's 1 a.m., I take a moment to imagine his Celtic-Germanic visage gazing at me adoringly, and I think to myself: *Not worth it, my darling girl – not worth it.*

I sometimes daydream about devoting my working life to food instead of my current job – telling strangers personal things. I've got a head for business and a bod for sin, and the food business has always intrigued me. I wouldn't like to work in a slaughterhouse and electrocute lambs for a living, or in an oats factory where I would have to pick out the jumbo ones from the pinhead ones all day long. The food world I dream about has no killing and no porridge in it, and is based largely on my perception of my sister Lilly's life.

Lilly is a food writer. She denies being a savant, but I struggle to come up with any other explanation for her innate flavour know-how. She takes a tiny bite of something, and can list the ingredients immediately. *Fennel seed!* she barks, or *wild garlic.* Lilly cooks and bakes and writes recipe books and columns. I imagine her work happens in a rural utopia, where she wanders into the kitchen, stands on the cool stone floor and says, to a blushing bunch of rhubarb: *Now, what am I going to do with you?*

Once, Lilly was going for a walk through the bird sanctuary near her cottage, looking for redcurrants – I'm not making this up; she is basically *Snow White* – when she saw a paper bag in the long grass. A sad part of this fairytale is that ignorant townsfolk sometimes throw their rubbish into the bird sanctuary, because they don't have song in their hearts. Listen up: the bag was moving! There was something alive inside it. Lilly's cup runneth over: she was sure it must be kittens. She pictured cute ones, with patches on their eyes and little fat tummies. She rushed over to open the bag. Glaring at her from inside sat a rat, busily gorging himself on some potato peelings. Lilly got a shock, but popped him into the pram, and brought him home to live with her anyway.

That very last part is untrue, but the rest is all completely factual.

Unlike most of us, Lilly did not shoot at the rustling paper bag. Instead, as I have said, she assumed it concealed a bunch of kittens looking for a new home. That she could even have the expectation of finding kittens as she went about her working day proves to me how lovely her job is. It's a real job, though. I know she has work to do like everyone else, and deadlines to hit too – like remembering to burp bottles of elderflower champagne four times a day.

I wonder what sort of food writer I'd make. Lilly works from home, which is something I excel at. I would stay in my pyjamas all damn day, simply popping on a chef's hat to denote work time. My signature dish would be anything I'd added dairy to.

One potential problem, however, is that I'm not very creative when it comes to cooking. When I look in the cupboard and find a jar of anchovies, a tin of coconut milk and an overripe pear, I pop them in the blender and hope for the best. I would also worry about myself in Lilly's job, because I sometimes go into a trance and eat entire things. You know how lots of cakes are traditionally served by the slice? I know that too, and I agree with it – in principle. It's just that sometimes it's better just to tidy up one side of a flourless chocolate cake by taking little slivers from it every few minutes, but then a droning noise starts in your head and before you know it, the cake has been 'tidied up' to nothing. Gone! It's like it wasn't ever there – except I now feel sick, worthless, and extremely giddy. So, no food business for me – just in case I end up eating the world.

I generally enjoy eating, except when I'm doing so in one of the aforementioned trances, or at a dinner party. Both are similar, in that they creep up on me in a peculiar, dull way and I always regret them afterwards. Dinner parties are the worst. Everyone must sit down in the same place all night and discuss food intolerances and the crisis in the Eurozone. Sometimes those evenings are such hard work that the whole thing becomes an image from a graphic novel in my mind: all of us sitting there with a collective thought bubble hanging over our heads which asks: *Is this it?* If the first half hour of a regular party is the hardest, the last half hour of a dinner party is definitely the most exasperating. Saying goodbye is painfully drawn out by politeness on all sides. The dream scenario would be to high-five the host and leave immediately after dessert. Doesn't the word 'tiramisu' literally translate as: *Let's get out of here*? No?

Having said all of that, my favourite thing to do is have dinner with friends in my house, or one of their houses, or in a restaurant, so go figure. And I will too.

Alright, I've come back from figuring – but stopped short of figuring it out. So far, all I have is that the difference between dinner with friends and a dinner party has something to do with:

- Who is there.

- How comfortable they are with each other.

- Who is in charge.

Anyway, far more interesting is the topic of eating dinner on your own. When I am eating dinner alone at home, it is tempting to make something quick and easy to eat 'on the go'. A pot of yogurt and a hurried piece of coley during an episode of *The Simpsons*, say – or a hundred pickled onions and a tin of sardines, while Googling my own name with varied spellings. I try not to do that, however. Instead I focus and make something good – snipe or hare – whatever is in season. I sit at the dining-room table and make sure to roster on the same number of staff as I would any other day. I take care of myself, don't you worry.

I often eat in restaurants alone. Because of my work, of course! My goodness, you'd keel over if you knew how many invites for dinner I receive each week! My mantelpiece is groaning with the weight of them, and that's just the e-mails! It's just that being a touring comedian generally involves me going to an urban centre, doing a sound check, having dinner alone, then telling jokes to between forty and a thousand people, depending on the economy. The dinner alone in a restaurant part used to be tricky, but I'm good at it now. You better believe it: a lone wolf has got to be self-contained. I am, and, in fact, I really like it.

65

The last time I went for dinner with a friend was in a tapas place. (Question: how many tiny dishes does it take to feel like you've had dinner? Answer: an impossible, infinite number – that is why you should always have something sweet in your bag, as a full stop to a tapas meal.) My friend and I were seated at a large communal table, with a big, lonely-looking businessman at the other end. I smiled at him as we sat down. Aren't I kind? Old Solitary-Wheeler-Dealer-Le-Roux didn't smile back. In fact, he stared straight ahead for the entire meal. He ate a huge board of cold meats slowly and drank a bottle of red wine quickly. He had his phone on the table and I saw, with my keen young eyes, that he was darting between Twitter and his text messages. In between sips of salami and bites of Montepulciano, he refreshed his screen constantly.

Now, I like texting as much as the next guy. And I love Twitter, mainly because Swizz Beatz follows me. Stop rubbing your eyes: you're not seeing things, you're not going crazy – you read right! The 'Party Up (Up In Here)' producer, the husband of R'n'B legend Ms Keys, the singer of 'Everyday (Coolin')' totally follows me on Twitter! Even so, I have a no-phone-on-the-table policy when I'm eating alone. I front it out and so should you, Old Chubby-Ballbreaker-Le-Roux. Don't peck at some bloody gadget, it makes you seem wretched! Be cool, look around, eat slowly – and people will think you're a mystery French girl with a lot on her mind.

I shouldn't be telling this guy what to do – or anyone else for that matter – but allow me to pontificate a tiny bit more. When it comes to eating, this is what I know for sure:

1. A breakfast high in protein and fat, for example some chicken and some nuts, will stand to you for a good four hours.

2. Eating in the dark/standing up/tidying cakes still counts as eating.

3. Sugar acts like your friend, but does really mean things behind your back.

4. Cream is the best, and don't let anybody tell you otherwise.

5. Maybe don't put cream in your breakfast.

That's it – you're welcome! *Bon appétit!*

Sneaky, like a sneak

My parents are properly country in their attitude to animals. My mother only appreciates functional pets: useful ones that lay eggs or catch rats. If a hen – even a good layer – sneezes more than twice, she's history. Our dog Shirley would sometimes lie dozing in the shade with her tongue hanging out, and my mother would scan her, with eyes free of sentimentality, and say in an unsettling tone: *She's getting very old*. We'd all clamour to save Shirley, by insisting that it was a really hot day and that, seriously, she was only six. My father is from a farming family: as a youngster, calving cows and herding bullocks was all in a day's work for him, so you'd expect him to be practical when it comes to animals.* Less easy to understand is the way he groups them all together – he sort of thinks all dogs are male and all cats are female. I am sure he knows this isn't the case but, despite years of correction, he still says 'he' when referring to a dog, and 'she' for a cat.

---

* For any greedy young farmers whose ears pricked up upon reading that, Dad didn't get the farm. So, if you were planning on getting with me or one of my sisters, in the hope of a bit of prime east Cork agricultural land – think again. All we have to offer is our bangin' bods and great attitudes.

As well as having loads of children and a dozen or so animals on a year-round basis, my parents hosted Spanish students every summer for the entire decade of the 1990s. The steps-of-stairs nature of my family meant that one of us was always fourteen, one was always fifteen – and so on. The Spanish students that stayed were usually great. I can't really remember too many of them individually, but collectively they left me with the impression that Spanish people are relaxed, smell really nice and like to eat late. They are all fourteen in my head too – making it hard for me to imagine a Spanish person working as a traffic warden or owning property.

In one terrible exception to the happy Spaniard experience, the kid we got one summer was crazy. I don't mean crazy, like: *I'm so crazy, I wrote U2 lyrics on my shoes.* I mean crazy, like Vatican City crazy: dangerous, secretive and dressed funny. On 1 June 1994, my father and I waited with other families to collect our new student. A huge group of Spanish teenagers had arrived into Cobh that year, all wearing big yellow backpacks and walking on tiny tanned legs. Clustered together, they looked like a harmless millipede moving slowly down the hill from the cathedral to the square, where a harried woman stood with a clipboard, shouting mismatched names, for example: *McLoughlin, McLoughlin – where are you, Margaret? This is your young fella: Hernando da Silva Torres.*

We took home a quiet, smiley boy about the same age as me, thirteen. His name was Santo. I had zero interest in boys at the time. I was too busy writing overly personal letters to political prisoners in East Timor. Our Spanish boy seemed totally fine, although he wore backwards baseball caps and my sister Ettie later swore that he looked *sneaky – like a sneak*. The weeks went by unremarkably, save for my mother sighing when Santo put dry Weetabix into his pockets so he wouldn't have to buy lunch.

Although thinking back on it, there was one peculiar incident involving our cat Phyllis and an apple tree. One night my brother was coming home late from sea scouts when he heard a sad meowing from the tree at the end of the garden. He shone his torch up and it seemed that Phyllis had managed to get her neck stuck in a Y-shaped branch – her plump little body dangled there, as she faced the sky. Oliver climbed up and freed her quickly. He brought her inside, and she seemed mortified.

We thought she might have slipped while she was stalking a bird along the branch, though she was not usually clumsy. That incident was what Oprah refers to as a *red flag*. Like when your husband says: *Honey, don't you think that looks a little slutty? I think you should change, immediately* – and you're wearing a wool twin set, and he used to be nice.

Our other cat's name was Chink. I realise how not cool this name is. Over time, Ireland has become exposed to other cultures, and with that change came my mother's brand new explanation of her choice of name for Chink: *Oh you see, he was like a chink of light, you know? In our lives*.

One evening we were all having dinner, except for Santo our Spanish guest, who was eating later. He was outside, playing basketball. In between doling out the tuna fish pasta bake, my mother looked out the window. Concern crossed her face as she said slowly: *Lads, look down there to the garage – what's Chink doing?* We all gathered around and peered across to the garage. The door was open and it was pitch black inside, with just a small patch of floor inside the door illuminated by the sun. Chink ran across that patch really quickly, twice. Suddenly, he was tearing around in clockwise circles, whizzing past the door again and again. He wasn't usually a very active cat – like most other cats, his days were made up of endless combinations of sitting, eating and lying down. *What is he like?* asked my sister Ettie, laughing, but suddenly she stopped laughing, as Chink started to levitate off the ground. *Cooooool*, said my brother. Chink could fly! He circled quickly around the garage, zooming past the doorway, faster and higher each time.

Then my mother said *Jesus Christ* under her breath and ran out the back door, across the yard and into the garage. She emerged less than twenty seconds later, with Chink in one hand. With her other hand, she pulled away the orange twine wrapped around his neck. Santo reluctantly trailed behind. He was beginning to cry. My mother pointed to the back seat of her car, and Santo got in wordlessly. Then she came inside, handed my brother the rasping cat and told him to get Chink some water and make sure he was able to drink it. She looked at my father and said darkly: *I'll get rid of Santo*. With that, she grabbed her car keys, ran outside, slammed the door, reversed down the drive and was gone. My brother said: *She's definitely going to kill Santo and put his body in the marsh*. Two of my sisters started crying. I was horrified by what Santo had done, and hugely impressed by what my mother was about to do. She was going to kill the killer!

In the end, she let him live. He just had to move in with an elderly couple with no pets for the final two weeks of his trip. Back in the kitchen, in what must have been the second biggest shock of Chink's day, my father took him onto his lap and rubbed his head gently. The cat gazed up at him, still panting, and listened as my father talked to him in a low voice: *You'll be grand, he's gone now and we'll mind you because you're the best girl.*

Something happening somewhere

In my giant family, each of us children had specific jobs every morning. *If we don't pull together* – my mother would say darkly – *this ship will go down*. My brother Oliver was in charge of the hens, my sister Ettie made the school lunches and I looked after the baby, Daisy. I would get her up, change her nappy and feed her mashed-up porridge. I don't know what the mass of girls in between me and Daisy did to earn their keep. They were too young to be effective really, so probably just did 'jobs', like counting teddies or folding facecloths. I was confident that I was great at my particular job, because Daisy laughed almost all the time, at everything. The sound of the toast popping up, the dog licking her hand: it was all just hilarious in her baby mind. Even when she was teething, or under the weather, all I had to do was pick her up and dance around the kitchen to pretty much any Annie Lennox song, and she would cheer up and start laughing again.

Daisy was an easy baby, and convinced me that I was a wonderful babysitter. I talked a lot of talk along those lines. *This gun's for hire*, I told everybody. Word spread like wildfire, and at fourteen years old, I became the one to watch in the local babysitting stakes. I was a triple threat – lots of younger siblings, giant glasses and absolutely no social life. The calls came flooding in. I gladly accepted all babysitting jobs on offer.

Just so we're all on the same page, by babysitting, I mean walking to a nearby home, seeing off the parents of that home, and then setting about eating all the snacks available, slowly and methodically, in order of how delicious they were. I babysat for a number of families right through my teens, and the children never woke up when I was there. Except for one time, when I went to one of my regular jobs and the family had their thirteen-year-old cousin staying with them for the weekend. I was a year older than her, but I wasn't sure if she knew that. We sat together watching TV and talking about our favourite lunches until 9 p.m., when I told her to go to bed and go straight to sleep.

If I was a parent, I don't think I'd employ a fourteen-year-old girl to guard my household and children, as I line-danced the night away in the local GAA club. When it comes down to it, what can a fourteen-year-old girl really do? They can count how many children are there and ensure that the number remains more or less the same throughout the evening. They can spot when the house goes on fire – but any Jack Russell worth its salt can do the same. Young girls' talents – drawing ponies and doing French plaits – are not compatible with taking care of a household for a night. I couldn't do first aid, or understand lisps, or spot the difference between a genuine uncle and a shifty-looking man popping in to collect the TV and jewellery for repair.

Ettie was a babysitter too, as was Lilly when she turned fourteen, and so on. On Sunday mornings my sisters and I would all sit around the table and compare notes. We talked about how pretty the mother looked going out, how drunk the father was dropping us home, what we got paid and the selection of snacks and videos on offer. We debated issues, such as whether getting paid IR£1.50 an hour, with all the Monster Munch you can eat, is preferable to getting IR£2 an hour, with just a bag of popcorn. You could just buy whatever pickled onion flavoured corn snacks you wanted with the extra cash – but we all agreed that we probably wouldn't eat them with the same wild abandon if we'd bought them ourselves.

Around the time of my babysitting heyday, Princess Superstar had a hit with a song called 'Bad Babysitter'. The lyrics included the line: *I'm a bad babysitter, got my boyfriend in the shower … I'm making six bucks an hour.* The part that always fired up my imagination in that song is not the boyfriend part. I didn't have a boyfriend in my teens.

When I was fourteen, I moved to an all-girls school – colloquially known as the Virgin megastore – and my only access to boys was on the train to and from my orthodontist's appointment once a month. Just after your braces have been tightened is not a great time to chat a fellow up, because it's tricky to enunciate words, and words are a key element of talking. Instead I would sit as close to the boys as possible, pretend to read *NME* and listen in on their conversations.

I'd phone my best friend Alison that evening and fill her in on what was going on in the world of these boys. (She alone could make out what I was saying through the squeaks and lisps caused by teeth being slowly hauled into place.) The boys' conversations were often about school or sports, or who was gay. Sometimes they were more interesting – like when they openly discussed which girls' schools were the sluttiest. Ours never got a mention. I liked one boy in particular because he didn't contribute much to the homophobic bullying, and, written in tiny writing on his schoolbag, he had: *The killer in me is the killer in you*. I wanted so badly to talk to him but he was completely unreachable. It wasn't just that I couldn't physically talk: it was that boys seemed as different to me as birds or lizards. It was like we all existed together on the same planet, but not in the same world. I could grab hold of them and try speaking English to them, but I knew I wouldn't be able to make them understand what I meant.

The impossibilities presented by Princess Superstar at the time pile up. I didn't have a boyfriend, and if I had, I wouldn't have wanted him to go babysitting with me because I'd have had to split my meagre earnings. And even if this non-existent boyfriend did come baby sitting with me, I doubt very much he'd have had a shower while we were there. I hated having showers when I was fourteen, particularly when there were Chickatees and Toffee Pops to be eaten. The main part, however, that I could not get over in the Princess's song was her casual reference to *six bucks an hour.* SIX? That was approximately triple what I was getting, depending on the exchange rate at the time.

When I was seventeen, I got the babysitting job of a lifetime. The summer I finished school, I went to work as an au pair for an Irish family in New York. That's right, world! Little Old Mimsie made it to the Big City! So you better watch out! I was beyond excited about my new life. No more parents telling me to eat my porridge; no more fields; no more sharing a room with a load of look-alikes. I would be free! And I had a few ideas of what that freedom would look like:

- Me, in an Erykah Badu style head-wrap, walking around Harlem high-fiving people, tagging walls and skipping through a fire hydrant's leaking waterfall before cooling off on a brownstone's steps and laughing with an elderly man in a cool hat.

- Me, inside a boardroom with a huge glass table, at the top of a huge skyscraper, wearing a black polo neck and eating sushi expertly, while laughing with some Japanese people also wearing black polo necks.

- Me, sitting in a café called Central Perk, holding a big mug with both hands and laughing with Jennifer Aniston and Matthew Perry.

What actually happened was as follows. I was collected from the airport by the mother of the family I was moving in with and her two youngest children. She drove us to a pretty suburban house a few miles outside of Rye, a town about an hour away from Manhattan.

I left my bags up to my room and started peeling potatoes for dinner. I loved the garbage disposal system in the sink and the huge fridge with an ice-maker, and I really loved the eight-month-old baby. Everything else was kind of a letdown. The older children were reeling from their last au pair's departure – from what I gathered, she had left unexpectedly. When I asked my boss about it, she simply said: *Oh, you know how unreliable the bloody Germans are.*

And I said *Absolutely!* – although I had never heard that particular accusation levelled at the Germans before. However unreliable Gerta had been, though, the children had clearly adored her. That's how I knew her name was Gerta: the three-year-old insisted on calling me that the whole time I was there. She also threatened me with the authorities, constantly. She would stand outside my bedroom door and yell: *Gerta! I'm calling the cops if you don't gimme more Froot Loops and come play Furbies with me!* There were too many children. If you're planning a family, take it from me: four children is too many. Go easy on yourself, just have one or two. One of the boys used to wet his bed every single night, and it was my job to change the sheets. I began to set my alarm for 4 a.m., lead him to the bathroom and then put him back into bed. My boss was thrilled when we reported dry sheets every morning for a week. I told her about my genius solution to the problem. She wasn't as pleased as I'd hoped – in fact she told me to stop doing that, because she needed to work on the underlying cause that the wetting was just a symptom of. I understood what she meant, but dreaded waking up to a soaked, upset child and another load of washing every morning.

When you're a live-in babysitter, you really get to see how a family lives. Their mistakes and triumphs are right there for you to examine, and it's fascinating. Be that as it may, I wouldn't recommend it. Save yourself the heartache and just watch a really well-made documentary instead.

I had every Sunday off. I went into the city then, with my wages in my hot little hand: at $150 a week, still not close to six bucks an hour. I went to see the sights in the greatest city in the world. When I say the sights, what I mean is, I would get a train from Rye to Grand Central Station, buy a subway token for $1.50, a giant bag of Doritos and settle down on the subway for epic people-watching sessions. I'm allergic to that particular brand of self-consciously quirky girls that seem to be everywhere these days: you know, the ones who want the world to know just how prone to whimsy they are. They come out with chestnuts like: *I love people-watching* – and I want to say: *I'm people – watch this!* And then break their ukulele over their heads and set fire to their little red shoes. Everyone loves people-watching: humans are curious by nature. So don't think you're charming me, young lady, with your handmade-looking jumper that you bought online.

So take it from me, I am not trying to be cute when I tell you that I sat on those trains on my days off and I people-watched harder than a motherfucker. I couldn't get enough of watching people. It went way beyond the usual furtive glances and brief imaginings of other's lives. I would examine them, trying to figure out who they really were, by gazing openly at their faces with an intensity that must have unnerved my subjects. If you've been living in a rural community on a tiny Irish island, waiting for your life to start, and you've just arrived in the only place for that to possibly happen, then of course you'll gaze hungrily at the people who are already there. Back home, I was dogged with the feeling that there was something happening somewhere, and that somewhere was New York. But now I was there, feeling the same way.

I would sometimes go above ground with a phone card and ring Alison back in Cobh. I'd make sure to call from a pay phone on a busy street, so she could hear the cars honking and the sirens blaring in the background. She'd fill me in on her new boyfriend and how the debs went and her summer job in the local pub, and I'd tell her about the three-year-old who was dominating my every waking hour, and the Jewish men with curls all down their cheeks I'd seen on the train.

When I got back to the house on Sunday evenings, my boss would ask me what I had done on my day off. I would tell her that I sat on the 'Q' all the way to Coney Island three times and spent the rest of the day on the 5. She seemed concerned at this, so I eventually started telling her that I went to look at the Egyptian jewellery in the Metropolitan Museum of Art, or to Ellis Island, or to Burger King.

One evening my boss told me she'd signed me up for a dance class at the community centre, so that I could meet people. It was a ballroom-dancing class, with eight elderly ladies and two even more elderly men. Well, it wasn't exactly a class. There was no teacher – they were just a group of pals who'd been dancing together since the 1960s and used the community centre. They hadn't had a new member in a long time, let alone a bulky teenager with two left feet and a funny accent. I liked the classes, though – except for one time, when I think I injured Max, the smallest, frailest man there. I got stuck trying to duck under his arm doing the Lindy Hop. The old people were very kind to me. One couple in particular, Cheryl and Ezra, would often drop me home and ask me questions about Ireland. They made me feel like I was interesting and exotic, as opposed to the odd one out. I would love to find them now and thank them for that.

Seventeen is a tricky age, wherever you are. I thought I was doing fine, but I can see now that I was struggling. I was very much on my own. I had been dying to get away from my family and do things my way, but these things hadn't worked out the way I'd imagined. There were no head-wraps or sushi dinners or *Friends*.

I stuck it out, though. When I wasn't looking after children, dancing with old people or staring at everyone else, I watched TV in my room. Having a TV of your own with thirty channels was a major coup for someone used to ten people fighting over three channels. I would prop myself up on pillows like a sickly Victorian and watch Comedy Central and The Food Network every night. My favourite show was *Two Fat Ladies*. It still is my favourite show. I loved how Clarissa Dickson Wright and Jennifer Paterson were so silly and funny and unselfconscious on screen. I also watched stand-up specials by Margaret Cho and Kathy Griffin. I had never seen stand-up comedy before, live or on TV, and I thought those women were incredibly funny and cool. I guess from then on, cooking and stand-up fused in my brain and that's why I forced my sister Lilly to cook while I told jokes at my first show at the Edinburgh Fringe Festival – and then tricked her into doing a TV version, which was *Fancy Vittles*. I'm glad something was happening during that vast tract of time in suburban New York, when my life seemed to be standing very still. I'm also glad I don't work as a babysitter anymore – but I sure do miss the snacks.

Dolphins have sharp, conical teeth

During my hilarious stand-up comedy routines, I sometimes panic and ask my audience: *Who am I going to talk to when you all leave?* Most people laugh, except the more tuned-in ones: they look concerned for a second and then laugh. I hope they don't remember what I've said later – I'd feel bad for making them think about me after the allotted time. Lots of comedians play video games or have sex with fans in their spare time, but I'm not dextrous or disconnected enough for either of those – yet. The like-minded among us meet and eat after our shows, so that's how I often find myself: eating greasy food in a new country after midnight with a bunch of neurotic guys. I've made some brilliant friends that way.

Snacking with other comedians definitely kept me going for about the first three years of life as a touring clown. Each city's museums occupied me too, and I knew I was really onto a good thing when I discovered foreign supermarkets. I don't like shopping centres and how they turn people into zombies: walking into each other with glazed eyes and emitting low groans about the injustice of sizes.

I love supermarkets, though, and can happily spend an afternoon in a new country meandering around the aisles. I examine all the cool products that we don't have in Ireland: fruit roll-ups, pumpkin in a can, horrifying fish, gem squash, Vietnamese basil, and whole fridges dedicated to grape-flavoured everything. I play house in my head. I imagine doing a weekly shop as part of my new life as a resident of Wellington or Edinburgh or Brooklyn, or even Adelaide. Adelaide is a sun-baked city in South Australia full of pick-up trucks and the people who drive them. It has a great indoor food market and a wonderful museum, but cheese and Aboriginal art can only keep a girl busy for so long. Three mornings, to be exact – and I was there for five weeks, doing a show at their annual arts festival. It was going fine – my stand-up was amusing more people than it was bewildering. I was staying up as late as I liked; I saw a koala; some smiley Australian ladies organised my schedule daily – and I had four months on the road ahead of me.

I was great at being on my own! One day I realised that, apart from the eighty strangers a night I was telling personal things to, I hadn't spoken to anyone in four straight days. I was enjoying the twenty-three hours of keeping myself to myself. I felt like a spy or a fugitive or an only child. I got into a routine: I slept late, read my book, watched *Oprah*, looked around the supermarket for a couple of hours, did my show, ate dinner, went back to my hotel, checked my e-mails but didn't respond to them, and slept again. I began to think of home as a lovely, distant memory. *Those people were so nice*, I'd recall dreamily, picturing my family and my friends in Ireland, but rarely answering the phone when they called. It was easy to just float along, barely touching down every now and again to have an exchange with someone in a café or a shop.

Before I knew it, though, my solitude turned into loneliness. The kind that scares other people. Uh-oh! I figured it out too late, in a Haigh's Chocolate shop. I was the only customer in there, and the girl behind the counter was about my age. *Potential friend alert!* screamed my heart. My head told me to steady on and play it cool.

What are these? I was enquiring about some large rodents made from chocolate.

Those are Easter wombats.

I laughed a high, tinkling laugh, and said: *Oh, in my country we have Easter bunnies mainly – rabbits.*

The girl pointed wordlessly to the shelf behind me, full of chocolate bunnies.

I nodded vigorously. *Yes. Like those! I'm Irish. I'm just in town for the festival.*

She asked if I liked Adelaide, reluctantly. She was just asking out of the minimum politeness required of her to work in a customer-facing job, but she sure unlocked the floodgates with that one!

Oh yes, it's good, I like it – but it's weird being away for so long, and I don't know what to do with myself really – what age are you? I'm twenty-five. She looked around nervously, and said she was twenty-four.

I said: *Oh my God, we're practically twins! Do you like working here? How d'you not eat everything?*

She smiled weakly and shrugged. It felt so nice to chat to someone! So I kept going. *I have a lot of sisters, they are so great – I miss them. Do you have any sisters?*

I think I even asked her if she played board games. The debacle lasted until another customer came into the shop, and she fled to help them. I tried to get her back by lingering awhile and eventually buying a huge chocolate wombat dressed for the beach. I commented on how funny it was that the wombat was wearing chocolate sunglasses and told her an anecdote about the time my parents left me at the beach by accident. She smiled tightly and wrapped the wombat up in lots of cellophane and ribbons, as if it was a gift for someone.

Back in the hotel room, I lay on my bed and tried to come up with a plan. No more ambushing shop workers! I would have to keep busy from now on, and stave off these outsider feelings. The chocolate wombat gazed at me, smirking through his shades. He was beginning to melt, so I quickly ate him right up.

Two months and four cities later, I found myself with three days off in New Zealand. At this stage I had begun to follow strangers around and build imaginary profiles of their lives. I set aside one day to marvel at the various breakfast cereals, canned meats and hair care products available for inspection in the local supermarket. I knew it would be wrong to use the rest of my free time to unnerve locals, so I decided to have some 'adventures and experiences', as advertised by the tourist office in Auckland.

Behind the desk at that tourist office sat a smiley, chubby lady in a navy cardigan. She ate a biscuit from a drawer as she planned two days' worth of activities for me. She also explained that the tourist season was almost over and arranged the brochures into two piles: ones with activities that were still available and ones I just missed. She handed both piles to me. Glacier walking and white water rafting were out, she dimpled, but I could try out her own personal favourite activity – taking the TranzAlpine train for 12 hours from the North Island to the South Island, and back again. Perfect!

I love train journeys: they suit me because I like to imagine I'm a melancholy French girl on her way somewhere, and over 12 hours I could really cultivate that persona. The brochure featured, as one of the trip's highlights, 'the famous TranzAlpine Express chicken curry'. Other selling points of the trip apparently included toilets in every carriage, and a potential muffin stop. *Tick, tick, tick*, went the boxes, *boom!* went my heart, and I booked my ticket.

The farmer's wife (I'm assuming, because of the wedding ring and rosy cheeks – although something told me she wasn't in love with him anymore) then looked at her computer screen and back to me again, beaming and saying: *Oh, wonderful news! The dolphin experience is still happening next week, so … you could swim with dolphins: a lifelong dream!*

I got carried away on Mrs Cuddle's wave of excitement. Although swimming with dolphins was never my lifelong dream, I heard myself saying: *Wow! Incredible! Book that too, one ticket, please, all the way there and back again!*

My lifelong dream is to master pull-ups, start a family with Michael Fassbender, and have Jennifer Paterson come back to life and be our private cook. However, the dolphin thing is many people's dream. Including sick people – and they know the wheat from the chaff. So I thought it would be churlish to turn down the opportunity. One thought did strike me, as I handed my credit card to Little Miss I-married-the-wrong-man-therefore-I-covertly-overeat-at-work. That thought was: *Maybe, considering my paralysing fear of fish, swimming in the sea with some big fish look-alikes isn't ideal* – but I dismissed it. Everybody knows dolphins are not fish, they are mammals, and I am not scared of mammals.

I put down the first day very happily: the supermarket did not disappoint. I found a whole range of cleaning products made from New Zealand lamb fat, and some sweets called 'Pineapple Lumps' that were very different to real pineapples. I brought some with me on the TranzAlpine train the next morning, to help me make friends. In the taxi on the way to the train, I decided that that would be pathetic and that I should try to be self-contained. I repeated to myself: *You're just a cool French girl with a lot to think about.* I would chat when chatted to, but not be needy and scare people.

The train was busy – most of the seats were occupied by elderly couples busily setting out flasks and lunchboxes, even though it was just 8 a.m. I was pleased to see them all: they were very much my demographic. I'm boasting now, but truly, elderly couples can't get enough of me. Maybe it's my baby face or our shared interests, or my conservative sensibilities. They know a kindred spirit when they see one sitting alone – that's for sure.

A pair of weathered New Zealanders sat opposite me and immediately introduced themselves. They were Barbara and Michael, and it was their fifth time making the same journey. They asked me where I was from and I said Ireland, and Barbara said that that was interesting, because her grandparents were both Scottish. Michael said the train was one of the best things in New Zealand, right up there with the All Blacks. He asked me about the English rugby team, and I explained I was Irish. He nodded his head, but in his heart he believed that I was just mixed up about my geography. They asked me what I did for a living.

Now, I hope you'll understand why I lied to these dear, friendly Kiwis. I don't like saying *I'm a comedian*, because of the inevitable disappointment that follows. I like to think I lie to save everyone the awkwardness, and not because I'm a sneaky liar. In fact, I've cut my lying right down in recent years.

I used to fib a lot as a teenager, just about small things. *Yes, I'm finished my homework, Yes, I'm on the pill* – that sort of thing. I thought it was fine because Holden Caulfield was a fibber too. I still slip into my deceptive old ways sometimes, when I'm not concentrating. Just yesterday, a taxi man asked me what was in my shopping bag, and I said a wedding present for my friend who was getting married in west Cork. I don't know where I got that from: it's completely false. Maybe I lied because of what *was* actually in the bag. It was a floral plate with gold edges, very frivolous and chintzy. I have a lot of old-looking, flowery crockery. I'm a disgrace for it. If you snuck into my kitchen and had a good peer into the dresser, you'd come to the conclusion that I was either very elderly or the owner of a tediously adorable café. More fool you! I am young* and I'm too full of street smarts to stand around making heart-shaped scones all day for women in flowery dresses and their predictably adorable babies.**

---

* In my heart, I am in my mid-to late sixties.

** Doing just that is secretly a dream of mine – hence the defensiveness.

So, I lied to the sweet couple and said I was a waitress. I used to be a waitress, have been loads of times. Indeed, in a variety of cafés and restaurants through the years, I was a terrifyingly good waitress. Coming from a co-dependent family meant I was able to anticipate what people needed, almost before they knew they needed it. Male customers appreciated my clumsy attempts at flirting, while my plain, open face didn't intimidate female customers, and one and all were charmed by my intense need to please.

An hour later, when we'd moved onto talking about Michael's new knee, my waitress story started to unravel. Barbara threw me a curve ball, you see – she asked what the menu was like in the restaurant. I said: *What menu? What restaurant?* I then saw their expressions turning from curious to concerned, and quickly rescued the situation by saying: *Oh, my restaurant? There are curries on it, but it's not an Indian restaurant – it's sort of French, but with some curries.*

As we journeyed slowly through beautiful woods and over snow-capped mountains, Michael got increasingly upset that I didn't have a camera. He kept asking: *You sure you don't have a camera, Doll?* I said that I was fine: I didn't want pictures. He said I had to have pictures to show my parents. I said I'd bought lots of postcards already, back at the train station – an accordion full of images, showing the various stops along the way. I showed him, and together we studied a close-up of the world's only alpine parrot: a dun-coloured, disappointed-looking bird.

Despite the postcards, Michael insisted that I needed some photos to bring home with me, to show I'd done the journey. His wife looked at me sadly and said: *You do, Doll – you'll be glad of them when you're back in the UK.*

The train stopped for ten minutes at a station called Arthur's Pass, so that everyone could get their photo taken with a sign saying *Arthur's Pass. Come on,* Michael said, and he got up slowly, leaning on his walking stick. *Let's go out to the viewing carriage and take a few snaps.* I said that really, it was OK, I was so cold and Arthur's Pass wouldn't mean anything to anyone back home. But they insisted that it was a crucial shot, so out we went. I waited my turn, frozen, and annoyed Michael by squinting into the camera. *We've gotta keep snapping – this girl's on her own, you see, and she needs to show everyone what she's been doing in New Zealand.* The people behind us had to adjust their hearing aids to make out what he was saying over the whistling wind.

Later, when the three of us sat together in the dining car and ate the TranzAlpine Express chicken curry (the one crowed about in the brochure), Barbara asked me how it stood up to the curry in my restaurant. I said: *What restaurant?* She narrowed her eyes a bit until I remembered my complex layers of untruths. I then said that it compared very well, but our chef didn't use as much coriander. That's the thing about spending twelve hours on a train with strangers: there's plenty time to really get among each other's lives. I still think about Barbara and bossy old Michael.

At 7 a.m. the next morning, I boarded a minibus driven by a blocky, scowling woman. I was the only one on it for the first fifteen minutes, but that didn't stop her using her microphone headset. *Just got one more hotel pick-up and we'll be off to Rotorua,* she boomed. When I asked her how many people were coming, she said: *Just two, and that's because it's actually past the end of season now – it's unusual for people to still be hanging around.* We stopped and collected a very old American couple. I helped the lady in and her hand was soft and tiny, like a chick. It took the pair ages to get onto the bus and settled. The driver rested her head against the steering wheel for a second, then said in a menacing way: *And we're off.* The old lady made a 'here-we-go' face at me, and I was very glad she was there.

We exchanged small talk for a minute or two, but it was difficult to hear over the amplified sighs of the driver. Also, I reminded myself, this was their holiday and I shouldn't inflict my company-starved self on them too much. So I sat down two seats away from them and looked out the window. The driver reeled off information in a bored tone that bounced off the minibus walls. *Quick fact about glow-worms for you guys: the fellas that burn the brightest are the hungriest.* In the beginning, myself and the Americans encouraged her, by saying *oh*, and nodding at each other but that seemed to irritate her. So we piped down and let her get on with it. Two-and-a-half hours passed in a long, slightly nervous heartbeat.

We got to Rotorua and were deposited underneath a sign with three arrows pointing in different directions – one to 'The Dolphin Experience', one to 'The Whale Watching Experience' and one to 'The Café Experience'. The American lady smiled a goodbye to me, linked her husband's arm and they slowly walked in the direction of The Café Experience. I was forty-five minutes early for The Dolphin Experience, so waited on a low wall. I spent the first twenty minutes missing

Michael and Barbara, and fighting my instinct to trail after the nice Americans and pretend they were my grandparents. Then my mind turned to the day's activity: swimming with dolphins. I spent the next twenty-five minutes looking at the choppy sea and trying not to think about who or what was rattling around inside it. As I say, almost daily, to anybody who will listen, even thinking about fish makes me shiver. I hoped I wouldn't see any that afternoon.

At noon I went inside, paid my money and joined the group. There were about twenty people, mainly English backpackers and a few middle-aged couples. We watched a video about how great dolphins are. As I watched them swim around on screen, I shuddered involuntarily. It showed dolphins speeding along, slicing through the water like fish-bullets. I started to get knots in my stomach. I hadn't thought about how like fish they were since that afternoon in the tourist office with Mrs That's-the-way-the-cookie-crumbles-in-my-lap. They are mammals but they look like fish, in the same way that tomatoes are fruit but look like vegetables. It began to dawn on me that I, a person who is terrified of fish, should definitely not swim with dolphins.

I shook the feeling off. I would be fine. I reminded myself again that dolphins are not fish – fish are mackerel and pike. And that people love swimming with them! It'd be crazy to turn back now, after the video and the safety talk and everything. These dolphin guys were charming and warm-blooded: not a million miles away, evolutionarily speaking, from Michael Fassbender. By all accounts, they were very sweet creatures. The voiceover was now saying that dolphins empathise deeply with humans. Sometimes, apparently, they even adopt people's emotions as their own. When depressed people swim with them, the next day the more sensitive dolphins can wake up with an 'oh, what's the point anyway?' feeling. Upon hearing this, the English girls crinkled up their faces and said 'Aww', and a middle-aged man squeezed his wife's shoulders as they shared a look. Fortunately, the narrator continued, the dolphins we were going to hang out with were wild and not overly exposed to human sadness, so they had a great attitude.

A woman wearing a Dolphin Experience T-shirt and flip-flops came and introduced herself as Kate, our dolphin guide. Then she talked to us about the very real possibility that we would not actually see any dolphins. She explained that they were of course wild creatures, and the area they roamed around was the actual ocean, so even the dolphin seekers in the special catamaran didn't know where they were all the time. Kate said that if they couldn't find them using their sonar machines, we'd get our money back and at least have had a boat trip. My panic – which had been rising steadily since I saw a dolphin on screen – began to subside. There was an out! The dolphins just needed to keep to themselves, and us humans could all relax and have a cup of tea in the café Experience.

After a couple of unnerving facts – dolphins can see behind them; dolphins have sharp, conical teeth – we were sent to change into wetsuits. The English girls shrieked and laughed at each other about how unflattering the wetsuits were. Changing into a wetsuit is definitely more fun with a group of friends. I found myself in that tricky position of doing an amusing thing with a group of people I didn't know, but who all knew each other. I kind of laughed along aimlessly, to show that I was fun and relaxed and recognised the humour in situations.

Wetsuits are pretty funny. I looked in the mirror and noted that mine failed to meet any of my criteria for a great outfit. I'm sure that the fashionistas among you are dying to hear my style secrets. Relax, Babes, grab a notebook and I'll let you in on my top three tips for a great outfit:

1. It's got to include underwear, in case you get in an accident or meet your DreamLover™.

2. It's got to have shoulder pads, because they make any woman look 15 per cent more powerful.

3. It must be completed by tribal earrings, to brighten up and distract from a plain face.

You're welcome!

With some difficulty, I zipped up the back of my rubbery onesie and waddled with the rest of the group to the pier. We boarded a wide, flat, dolphin-seeking catamaran. It was drizzling and the sea looked like it wanted to be alone. Kate, however, was full of optimism as she handed out binoculars and told us to shout if we saw any movement at all. We travelled far, far out to sea. Kate said the boat was going to zip around to the dolphins' favourite locations, and that we were bound to catch them. It's not like there are libraries or Mexican restaurants under the sea, so I wondered why they'd prefer one spot over another. I didn't ask, though, I just pretended to look through the binoculars.

Almost immediately, I saw a huge school of dolphins breaking through the waves on my side of the boat. I felt a rush of terror. I put down my binoculars wordlessly and began to plot a way of distracting a boatload of people from seeing the one thing they were longing to see. But my face betrayed me. This always happens. My face is so expressive that my sisters can tell what flavour ice cream I'm thinking about at any given moment. One of the English girls looked at me, then straight out to where the dolphins were. She screeched. I cursed her.

The boat followed the dolphins and we all took up positions along the back deck, ready to jump at the sound of the horn. Suddenly, the water was alive with them, all around us. Everyone was giddy with excitement, but I absolutely did not want to jump into that grey water with its big, irregular waves. I was furious at myself for being so scared. This was a once-in-a-lifetime chance; I was on the other side of the world; I was a grown woman in a wetsuit. And besides, dolphins were just mammals.

I instructed myself to cop on and jump in with such authority that I did – immediately. I jumped before the boat had stopped or the horn had gone. My first thought was that the water was like knives, my second thought was *SHARK!* I saw a shark under the water: the fin, the flank, the flat eye on the side of the horrific head, taking me in. I tried to calm myself by taking deep breaths, but they quickly turned into large gulps of sea water. I got my head above water just in time to see the boat disappear, and to realise I'd jumped too soon.

A wave tucked me under the quilt of the sea again, and I saw through stinging eyes that I was surrounded not by sharks, but by dolphins. They were standing up casually, smiling at me. Apart from the freezing cold and the intense fear, here were two things I hadn't anticipated: that the dolphins would be vertical under the water; and that they would laugh as they tried to kill me.

One of them levelled itself and swam towards me, fast. It swirled under my legs and I felt its firm fish body. Under water, nobody hears you scream. The dolphins rushed at me, brushing off my sides and turning me over, swishing past my hands as I tried to paddle. Of all underwater creatures, dolphins are surely the most malevolent.

I kicked and spluttered and tried to remember how to swim. I totally could not breathe. I kept thinking how unfair it was that these dolphins were going to drown me, but that everyone would think it was an accident. In what I assumed to be my final moments, no Super 8 reel of beautiful memories flickered through my mind. I didn't remember my father going around the table and covering our small heads with his big hands and kissing us on the foreheads, or my cat's slow blinks, or a brilliant boyfriend reading out loud to me one warm city morning. I simply thought, again and again: *These psycho fish are going to drown me and get away with it.*

I tried to shout, but couldn't make a sound. I finally remembered that, back at the orientation video, Kate had told us that if we got into trouble, we should put one fist straight up in the air. Just do the Black Power salute, and the boat would come and pick us up. As the dolphins continued to ram me and giggle, I used one arm to hold up the other, and struggled between waves to keep it up in the air. While I couldn't see them, I hoped that surely someone on the boat would see me. They did, and I eventually heard the boat approaching. The dolphins, predictably, fled the scene.

I couldn't muster up the strength to climb back on board, so I just clung onto the ladder. Kate kept saying: *Up you get! Come on, nearly there, you'll be fine.* She said it in a chirpy but anxious tone, the sort of tone you'd use to coax an aging relative into a nursing home. I couldn't move, so she climbed down the ladder and hauled me up on deck herself. I lay there for a minute, curled up like a fern. A vomiting fern. She asked if I was pregnant and I shook my head. She said that dolphins are the midwives of the sea, and that it seemed to her that they were trying to help me. She looked at me hopefully. I turned my face away and noted numbly that, of the row of brightly coloured life vests stacked under the seat, there was just one red one.

Back on dry land, I got shakily onto the waiting minibus. My eyes were burning from the salt water, my hair was matted and, understandably, I smelled of vomit. Despite this, I sat one seat closer to the Americans. The wife peered over the seat, through her huge bifocal glasses and asked: *How was your dolphin experience, little one?*

Great, thanks! I said, and started to cry.

My eyes are up here

Last year I wasn't allowed to visit my brother in Mongolia because I was in danger of going into a thyroid storm. Who knew my life would be so exciting? That I'd have a brother in Mongolia! That something that sounds like a meteorite shower might happen in my actual body! That I would one day have a medical condition so important, a doctor would actually phone me on my mobile and ask if I had travel insurance!

My brother Oliver has read the *National Geographic* magazine since he was four. He's also always been really easy-going – to the point of being almost impossible to rile up. I know exactly how to enrage my sisters within thirty seconds, and vice versa. But it's different with Oliver. Sometimes I call him 'Old Rosebud Lips', and he looks perturbed – but that's as far as it goes. He really has a dream pout: so perfect and plump. You know how, when you sip a pint of stout, your lip imprints are left on the foam, like a ghost's kiss? Well, when Oliver does it, there's a pretty little Cupid's bow-like imprint on the pint. When I do it, all I leave is a small, straight dent, like someone has dropped a coin in sideways. I have a little line mouth, one a lazy animator would draw on a character with no dialogue.

I've always felt like my mouth doesn't match my personality. It's the mouth of a bitter schoolteacher, hardened by years of failed love affairs and professional stagnation. I'm the kind of person who makes mix-tapes of soothing music for my pregnant sister without being asked: I'm sound and thoughtful. I'm not the kind of person who slaps dyslexic children when they misspell the word 'embarrassed', despite what my thin lips would have you believe. It's not fair: I'm female and need lips like Oliver's to attract mates. And yet, I do not have lips, so am forced to draw a big mouth over my tiny one with red and pink pencils each morning, before everyone else wakes up.

When Oliver was offered a job in Outer Mongolia, a combination of going with the flow and a sense of adventure made him take it. He moved far away to work in the mines, much like the father in *The Little Princess*, although Oliver didn't place me in a Victorian boarding school. And, instead of rubies and a charming manservant, he sent me home dried horse meat that I didn't eat.

I booked my flights to visit him and spent weeks reading up on local customs. I learned that I should never refuse an offer of fermented mare's milk, and that when Mongolians see a shooting star, they think someone is dying, and so spit over their shoulder and say: *It's not my star!* I was ready.

My ticker, however, had other ideas. I call my thyroid my ticker. This confuses doctors because for most people, their tickers are their hearts. The first clue I got about having a thyroid condition was given to me on the street by a wonderfully pass-remarkable stranger. A lady at a cash machine looked at me and said: *I hope you don't mind me saying, but your throat is swollen and it looks like a thyroid problem* – then she wandered off. I didn't mind, not at all. I was too busy being stunned – nobody talks to each other at cash machines! It's sacred time you spend with yourself and your four most precious digits. I've tried to engage with people at cash machines, and even with my winning personality and purely helpful intentions – *There's only fifties, you guys – just letting you know, it's only fifties today* – people avoid eye contact and look uneasy.

So I went to the doctor and was told that my thyroid was twice the size it should be, which meant that it was the size of four thumbs instead of two. (The doctor never specified who owned the thumbs.) I could feel that it was swollen, but not in a dramatic way. My throat didn't puff up like a bullfrog's. I'm glad of this because I am unmarried. Although you just never know what people are into. Convention states that a lot of guys are attracted to girls with bodies shaped like Coke bottles, and faces shaped like hearts. And women are supposed to go for men with triangle torsos and square-shaped heads. Me? I prefer a man with a figure like an oil drum and a star-shaped face. Maybe one day I'll meet someone who can't keep his eyes off my slightly swollen neck. That's how I'll know he's 'The One' – by The One, I mean a potential boyfriend, not Satan. The One's gaze will linger on my thyroid, time and time again, and I'll have to say to him, giggling: *Hey, Buster, my eyes are up here.*

It would be sort of nice to have some outward signs of my struggle. I know how mentally ill people feel now, because their diseases are invisible too. If someone cuts their cheek while shaving (that's not happened to me yet – touch wood), or breaks their wrist waving goodbye sarcastically to someone they hate, at least there is visual evidence that garners them sympathy. Nobody will sign my throat because it's not set in plaster of Paris. If my thyroid did balloon right out, it would be unfortunate, but at least it would be evidence of illness. Also, it would be a handy way for people to tell me apart from my sisters. *Oh you know Maeve, she's the one with the curly hair* – lowering their voices and checking to see if I'm around – *and the giant neck.*

The doctor suspected a delightfully titled condition known as Graves' disease and asked if I'd been experiencing any other symptoms, like anxiety or muscle weakness. I told her that in my family, it was a running joke to make a big pot of tea, then watch as I struggled to pour it. I told her that I didn't suffer from anxiety but that I did worry about death – my own and that of each of my loved ones – on an almost constant basis. I'd assumed this was caused by the introspective nature of my job. The doctor explained that, normally, people – even comedians – only worry about death at certain times, like when they're at a funeral or when they've been left on their own for too long.

To explain just how anxious people sometimes get when they have Graves', I will tell you about an acceptable clinical diagnostic method. It goes like this. To someone who's presented with a suspected case, the doctor says: *I'll be right back* – then pretends to leave the room. They actually just open and then close the door, and hide for a second. Then they scream *Boo!* loudly into the patient's ear. If the patient jumps out of the chair, it's probably Graves'. These aren't eight-year-old clown doctors either, they are qualified adults.

My no-fun doctor didn't try to give me a fright – she just asked me more questions, this time about how I was sleeping. I explained that I wasn't, that I was spending my time more productively, lying awake and planning other people's lives for them.

In the end, she took some blood tests, and phoned me three days later to say it was definitely Graves' disease. She told me not to go to Mongolia in case of a thyroid storm, which is when your ticker goes so baloobas that you have to be in a First World country.

So I phoned Oliver and told him I wasn't allowed to visit him in his new land. He tried to make me feel better about missing out, by saying things like: *I was actually thinking, everyone slurps their tea here, Maeve – you'd just hate it.* I do hate mouth sounds. I text complaints to radio stations if the presenters make too many mouth sounds. One memorable afternoon on the train from Cork, I moved three times because people near me were eating crisps and bananas. While I was glad to avoid the tea slurping, I felt pretty sorry for myself when I thought about all the good stuff I'd be missing out on. In the course of my research, I had discovered that Mongolians have, hands down, the cutest babies in the world. To intensify the cuteness, they swaddle them, creating little stiff packages of adorability for us to behold. No gawking at Mongolian infants for me though – I was staying in Dublin to get more tests done.

That was sort of fun too. Something about a medical professional focusing all of their concern and attention in my direction makes me feel giddy and important. Maybe that's because I'm from a big family, or maybe I have a personality disorder. It's just so nice, how they look at you with furrowed, quizzical brows and highly educated minds. I can sort of understand now why people exaggerate their symptoms or stick darning needles into their own brains – anything to get a doctor interested in them. Or, even better, *a consultant*. I am ashamed to admit that I got a real thrill out of those old guys in glasses who smell like money. To hell with interns and GPs: give me the golfers, the fine wine drinkers, the big Daddies of the HSE, and I will fib my little ticker out to captivate their expensive attention.

My least favourite test was the MRI scan. I showed up on time, registered with a sullen nurse, followed the lines painted on the floor to the correct waiting room and waited there for two hours. My name was called, I put on a paper robe and was wheeled into a metal tube for half an hour, fighting panic and listening to the radio. The worst part was the radio. The nurse offered me headphones, just as I was being inserted into the tube – she said they'd be a good distraction from the clanking noises. I hadn't realised there would be clanking. I also hadn't realised what time it was, and was devastated to hear what was on the radio – one of those lunchtime shows presented by loutish guys who talk about soap operas and football, and have a girl in studio whose exclusive purpose is to laugh at their jokes and say things like: *Guys! That is TOO far.* Irritating at the best of times, let alone when you're lying in a coffin, not allowed to move and it's being pumped into your head. I thought about pressing the panic button and asking them to change the station to Lyric fm – but I resisted, aware that it was not really an emergency and that, besides, they would probably just be repeating a Coffee Concert I'd heard before.

I'm all better now, but Oliver doesn't live in Mongolia anymore, so I missed my shot. Did you hear that, ladies? Old Rosebud Lips is back in town!

In case you're wondering how I got cured, I'll tell you. I took lots of thyroid medication and changed my diet and lifestyle. Boring! Also, I got a silk scarf and tied it super-tight around my neck where my thyroid is, like an air stewardess. Then I sprayed Chanel No. 5 directly onto my throat and shrank my old ticker that way.

Just clowning! I dress like a small boy, what business would I have with a neckerchief? And I didn't try the perfume thing either: it's not exactly a scientific idea. Also, I don't trust people who wear a lot of perfume or aftershave. It just means that they're not brave enough to wear stupid clothes or hum loudly. Instead, they take a sneaky route to your attention. I resent this, because I am especially susceptible to the power of smells. If I was a lamb and my mother died, you could totally trick me into believing any old ewe was her, by putting my dead mother's pelt on said ewe. My olfactory senses are suckers, and I wish people wouldn't take advantage. Hey, Teenage Boy! Stop tricking me into thinking you are a sophisticated old man who swims in the sea and smokes a pipe! My nose has built up a profile of you that your body can't cash.

I don't know why I got Graves' disease, it just happened. The Victorian doctor who discovered it, Robert James Graves, believed it came on after a traumatic event. He was all like: *Whence the lady was throwne from her steed of a hurry, the fright crystallised in her throat and served to worry her henceforth.* Or something. I don't agree with his theory. The worst thing that happened to me in the previous eighteen months was that a bird flew into the house and I had to catch it with a tea towel. My mother thinks you get diseases from not returning to your family home at every available opportunity. I don't know about that either, and doing so too often can bring on a stroke. Anyway, I'm fine again. (Chorus of men: *OH, MERCY – YOU'RE FINE ALRIGHT!!*) These days, when I see a shooting star, I make sure to spit over my shoulder then yell: *That's not my star!*

What's so funny?

Who doesn't love a good laugh, eh? I said: WHO DOESN'T LOVE A GOOD LAUGH, EH?

I'll tell you who: me, that's who. I don't love a good laugh, oh no, indeed I don't – not when it's absolutely uncontrollable and strikingly inappropriate. Like in the following instances:

- The first time I had a meeting with my accountant. We sat in a boardroom and talked about my tax return for that year. It suddenly dawned on me that I was an adult, paying to having a financial discussion with another adult, and that one day we would both grow old and die. I immediately burst out laughing. The accountant initially thought I was laughing because he had just said: *I mean, it's not* The Wizard of Oz *– you need a business account too.* He laughed a bit, and gamely said: *That's true, you know: it's not* The Wizard of Oz. I shook my head but couldn't talk through the unstoppable barks of laughter. I put my head in between my knees, but nothing worked. I raised my hand to apologise to him, and ran from the room, closing the door on his bewildered face. I laughed long and hard in the bathroom, got it together, dried my face and went back into the boardroom. Then I saw the two cups of coffee and the paperwork, and promptly lost it again.

–   Almost every time I argue with my sister Raedi, I start laughing. It is unhelpful. We live together and I use her stuff all the time. For the most part, she understands that I prefer the feel of her coat, or the light in her bathroom, or the way her phone doesn't cost me a penny.

Sometimes, after a marathon singalong-as-you-cycle-to-Sandyford-Industrial-Estate session with my girl Alicia Keys, Raedi flips out and says things like: *Maeve, you never charged my Nano after you used it, and now I can't use it for my class – so you are not taking it again.* That makes me laugh, nervously at first, then full throttle. This drives her crazy, and she asks: *What's so funny?* And I say, between slapping my leg, and snorting and gulping: *Nothing – I don't know, sorry!*

When I recover myself, I tell her that I'm laughing because I'm scared that she will leave me. For some reason, that makes her annoyed again. And of course, that makes me laugh all over again.

–   I was doing a gig with the singer-songwriter Jamie Lawson, around the time of his hit single 'Wasn't Expecting That'. It's a cute song about falling in love unexpectedly, having kids unexpectedly, and then dying unexpectedly. It's a real tear jerker at the end: the bit where the woman dies.

I watched the song's video recently and that bit is so sad: Lawson himself sort of cries as he sings it, but somehow soldiers on and delivers the lines. It's almost like he's so lost in the story that he forgets the camera is there, like Boyzone do in the video for their No. 1 single 'Gave It All Away', released after the death of Stephen Gately. Black-and-white shots of them writing letters to him in fountain pen are mixed with images of them weeping – it's quite something.

I hadn't actually heard 'Wasn't Expecting That' until Jamie Lawson was sitting on stage in front of me, singing it. When he reached the part where the nurses tell her 'it' has come back, and follows it up with the refrain about not expecting that, I had a sudden image of a tiger attacking an old lady. I exploded with laughter. I don't even think tiger attacks are funny, or diseases for that matter. I don't know why I was laughing, I just know I could not stop and I ruined the incredibly poignant moment for everyone there and I wasn't expecting that.

A great way to freshen
up a family

My parents have been fostering children since 1999. I want them to get a range of merchandise, stamped with *Fosterin' and Lovin' It – Since <u>Before</u> the Recession*. You know – T-shirts, maybe mugs, small things like that. But they won't. They think that would be tacky. Yet I ask them if my T-shirt with a picture of Bruce Springsteen on the back and the statement *The Only Boss I Listen To* on the front is tacky and they assure me it's not. Hypocrites!

Fostering is a trick used in soap operas to make families more interesting and bump up the potential for new, troubled characters. It is definitely a really great way to freshen up a family, but that's not why my parents do it. They do it, I think, because their hobby is collecting children and fostering is a civilly endorsed way of doing just that. They mainly take children under ten, usually girls, for short-term placements.

People ask my mother about how fostering works, and she tells them that the ideal outcome is the child being able to return to their birth mother. A huge proportion of people then stick out their bottom lip adorably and say: *You see, I would love to foster, but that's the part that gets me – I just couldn't do it. I wouldn't be able to give them back.* I always imagine them cupping an oversized mug with both hands and giving a little sad smile after saying that. They are basically telling my mother that she is lucky to be a robot with no capacity for emotion, while congratulating themselves on caring too much, which is just enough to do precisely nothing.

Also – and this is quite important – everything ends. In the early stages of a relationship, or an idea or even a bowl of ice cream, I sometimes catch myself thinking: *Maeve, you dope, where will you be when this is gone? Only worse off than you are right now, because you will be missing it!* I have to vanquish that thought and get on with the kissing or the writing or the eating, because what else can I bloody do?

My mother also gets asked what foster children are like. The answer, of course, is that they are like all children. I think of my little foster sisters, collectively, as a combination of happy, quiet, robust, hilarious, annoying, in-the-moment and supremely cute. Some of them like chickpea curry and soda water; others prefer chicken nuggets and tea. Some like putting on plays where they die dramatically at the end; others like watching documentaries about space travel. Obviously, they have often had a trickier childhood than, say, me.

Here were the main things concerning me circa 1988:

- That Roald Dahl would die and therefore stop writing books.

- That one or all of the cats would have kittens in a secret location that we would never find.

- That Bob Marley was dead.

111

Here are some of the things that have concerned my foster sisters through the years:

- That they will get to go home but that would mean not seeing my parents' dogs anymore.

- That they will have to start a new school in the middle of the year, again.

- That the other kids are crap at playing 'Social Worker'.

I like seeing new small girls sleeping in my childhood room and reading my old books. I hope they're having a good time. When I visit, I help them with their homework until they are about six or so, then it genuinely gets too difficult for me. In every way except my age, I am like a child-aunt to them. I do their hair and make fart jokes, so we get along great. It is their home now, not mine anymore. I am an interloper, disrupting their routine of school, snack, dinner, snack, garden, snack, bedtime.

I left home at seventeen and was replaced later that week by a bulldog with digestive tract issues, so I'm not sentimental. I'm a time traveller, watching a fresh batch of smallies get raised up by the same parents using the same methods, with the same mistakes and victories along the way. It makes my parents seem ageless, somehow. Well, that and the fact that they have both had *extensive* cosmetic surgery. Between you and me, my father's eyelids don't close anymore, and he's got that catty look you see on actresses of a certain age. He says it's worth it, because the construction industry is so bitchy towards middle-aged guys.

If you find yourself being fostered by my parents, here is some information that will help you make an easy transition to being a Higgins-household member. (This may also be helpful to people hoping to get civil-partnered to one of us. Yes I'm talking to you, Michael Fassbender!)

- At the dinner table, my Dad doesn't ask you to pass things to him. He just gazes at whatever it is he wants and you have to guess – kind of like the man in *The Diving Bell and the Butterfly*, but not French.

- At a certain time of day, when the sun is highest in the sky, you'll find me and my other fair-skinned, dark-haired sisters hovering near mirrors brandishing tweezers – and you mustn't ask why.

- When the phone rings, whoever fails to scream *Bags not getting it* has to answer it.

- Do not bring margarine into the house.

- Watching TV during the day is a sign of a depressive.

- Everyone gets jacked up on tea brack at around 10 p.m.

- We are not allowed to make my mother laugh when she drives, because she can't see the road when she laughs.

I think my parents are great. Apart from creating from scratch

a number of luminaries like me, and fostering many more legends among children, they successfully tricked each one of us into thinking we were their favourites. This emerged only last year, late one night after we had all watched *Seven Brides for Seven Brothers*. We were in our tiny sitting room, stacked on couches, wedged under the coffee table and lying on the floor, with the unmistakeable scent of sour cream and onion Pringles in the air. It was the same Saturday night we'd been spending for twenty years, so I don't know what brought on the discussion.

Oliver just suddenly said he had known since he was six that he was the favourite child. He cited evidence around our parents backing him up on a UFO sighting he had lied about. That started a big argument: the younger ones among us said they weren't even born when Oliver was six, so my parents couldn't have made an informed choice at that time. I remained silent for a while, but when Raedi dredged up the time when she had learned how to swim and got a new prayer book for her efforts, I was forced to bust out my truth about how I am, in fact, the number one most loved and prized child and that the evidence was irrefutable:

Exhibit A: When I was a small baby and began to cry one night, my father came running to comfort me. He stumbled on a rug and broke his toe but ignored it and kept running. Nice work, Pops!

Exhibit B: My mother once told me that, of all of her children's mental health, she worries most about mine.

No matter how much we cajoled and threatened my parents that evening, they won't confirm their favourite. Crucially, they didn't deny it was me. Sometimes I overhear my mother asking Raedi on the phone how I am, *really*. That's how I know I've still got it. Raedi frowns when she gets asked that, and says: *Mammy, ask her yourself – she's always bloody fine*. As a bit of fun, I hug my knees and rock back and forth on the ground and mime cutting my own hair with wild eyes. Raedi rolls hers up to heaven and leaves the room. You can do that now, with phones being mobile and all.

We're moving in together as housemates!

He's what you should know:

1. We should be open with each other

Because I work mainly at night-time, either as a comedian or an exotic dancer, I spend most of the day at home. This is when you will be at work. I have things to do during the day too – don't get me wrong. I go online and look at photos of desserts, I do a bit of writing and I sometimes hang out with friends who are unemployed, but have yet to emigrate.

Some days, when I've seen all the cake the internet has to offer and even that girl I didn't really like from yoga has gone to London, I get a bit bored and find myself in your room. Don't worry about this. I don't exactly poke around. I stick my head in and have a look. I like seeing what other people have on their bedside lockers, which books they're reading and how many pairs of jeans they own. Half the time I don't even know I'm doing it. Raedi figured it out when she got back from work and noticed that all her toiletries had their lids off. She asked me if I had anything to do with it. I thought really hard and finally remembered that I'd

116

spent about forty-five minutes that afternoon smelling all the different bottles of serums and lotions in her bathroom. I must have gone into an even deeper trance and forgotten to replace the lids. Isn't it funny how that happens?!

2. House guests are very welcome

I have a hard time with visitors. By all means, invite your friends over. Just know that when it comes to new people, I'm a little demon. I will either dislike them on sight or else want to steal them from you and make them my friends. The former is easier to deal with – just ignore me as I sit in judgement. The latter, watch out. If I come across a person I like, I am relentless in my pursuit of them. I use flattery, jokes, baking, my butt – anything at all – to win them over. You will be powerless to stop me, so maybe just meet them in a café or something rather than inviting them over.

3. Maybe you should just pretend to be allergic to cats

If you don't like Little Edie, please don't pretend that you do. I'm not even sure if I like her myself. She's not fluffy or cross-eyed. she doesn't go limp when you pick her up. She is unfriendly and plain and tough-looking. I love her, of course, because she's all I've got. I understand if you don't feel the same. It's awkward for me, for you and for Little Edie when you act like you enjoy being around her. You can tell me you think she's cute, in a scrappy way, but I will think you a liar. I can tell by your strained voice and her tense body language that you are not keen on her company, so please don't imagine that you are fooling anybody by trying to stroke her enthusiastically, then fake-laughing when she scrawls you.

4. It's not always possible to talk to each other

I love a chat party as much as the next guy, but sometimes, especially after gigs when I've used up all my words, I have to keep my trap shut. The only way to pull me out of the slough of talked-outness is by addressing me in the voice of a Prohibition Era gangster. I don't know why, but if you say something along the lines of – *Say Mimzi, what's eating you? And tell me this, what's a fella gotta do to get a Waldorf salad around here?* – I'll immediately get a wiggle on.

5. We don't have to share *everything*

I tell myself that I am not a materialistic person, but when it comes down to it, my food storage containers are a really important part of my life. Please don't think you can just use them to freeze your leftover moussaka or whatever other godforsaken morsels you've decided not to throw out. Yes, we share things like the colander and the spatulas, but those stacking boxes are mine. When you want to use them, you need to ask me first. If I say yes, you must allow me to select the best one for the task at hand, or else you'll do it all wrong. I've been building up my collection for years, and though they don't look like much, those little boxes are my flimsy heroes. I have a favourite: it's a 0.75 l capacity clear rectangle with a built-in rubberised seal and four locking tabs. Maybe you think I'm pathetic for having a favourite lunchbox. If so, you're out of the gang. Friendship terminated. We are worlds apart. If you understand, I'll tell you more.

This box is obedient and trustworthy, it fits into my backpack perfectly and the lid has never come off unexpectedly. By filling it with tuna salad or beef jerky and nuts, I have successfully been able to resist the siren song of the scone-in-town, that calls to me the way a naughty mermaid calls to a lonely sea-farer. We do well to resist the provocative moaning of mermaids and scones, because they both promise unbounded joy, but how do they leave us, only forlorn? And with a whistling wind. That's why I can't bear to think of my best box, my helpful pal in the battle against the scone-in-town, lying in the dark of a freezer drawer for years, getting stained orange from the obnoxious aubergine mess you've put in it ... So just check with me first, OK?

When I hit the big time, the first thing I'm going to do is buy a new 28-piece set of BPA-free plastic containers that resist stains and odours, and come with easy-find lids. Maybe I'll be less precious with them, but I doubt it. Moot point anyway, because when I hit the big time, I won't need a housemate. I plan on being as wealthy and incredibly isolated as Kanye West himself.

We have a good time ... don't we?

On our birthdays, our parents would take us – just the birthday child, alone – to dinner in the Tung Sing Restaurant in Cork city. Those annual spring rolls and glasses of Fanta are probably why I've got such a sophisticated palate and cosmopolitan outlook today. Being alone with my parents was an incredible feeling. On my eighth birthday, in the car to the restaurant, I actually became light-headed from trying to come up with increasingly outrageous stories to tell them. I had to stop talking and breathe into a bag.

I couldn't have handled that kind of attention year round. I would have exploded under the pressure. So, on balance, I'm glad to have millions of siblings. There's something brilliantly comforting and quite addictive about being surrounded by a large set of faces almost identical to your own. As a child, my siblings made me feel invincible – how could I end, when there are so many of me?

When I was small, I had two predominant daydreams involving my sisters. One went like this: we would be us, but a tropical version – wearing denim shorts and a number of leis, walking along a beach. Not an Irish beach, where you have to wear shoes because of shaley rocks and dark green seaweed fronds – an exotic beach with white sand and palm trees. Then we would meet Michael Jackson and he would say that we were great dancers, better than him and his brothers, even. That was it: the whole daydream lasted about ten seconds.

In my other, more melodramatic, daydream, I could stay inert and glassy-eyed for about forty minutes, imagining different scenarios which all began with a doctor presenting me with a choice.

Your sisters all need your organs, he'd say.

And I'd say: *No problem, doc, take 'em!* I'd be thinking he meant maybe one kidney or just a corner of my liver.

He'd say: *You don't understand, kid, they need your brain and your heart, as well as your spleen and things like that. The whole lot … or else the girls will die before they get married!*

So I'd have to decide whether I wanted to give my sisters my brains and skin and end up just a shell of a girl, or dead. Tears would actually fill my eyes, as I struggled with my hypothetical choice.

Sometimes the doctor would narrow it down to one sister, particularly if I'd had a fight with them earlier that day. He would always mention the getting married part as a deadline. I usually decided I would miss them too much if they died before they got married, so I would do the business. The doctor would clap me on the shoulder and prep me for surgery. My sisters would line up along the hospital corridor and say things like: *Are you sure, Maeve? Don't feel like you have to, now!*

I'd do a brave little smile and they'd be delighted with me, but appropriately sad too. When I snapped out of my trance, I would tell my sisters I loved them and make them shake my hand and say: *You and me, against the world!* They hated when I went all maudlin like that, and to this day they get freaked out by the intense way I stare at them. They give out to me when I say I feel like we're all the same and we never separated, that we're just like one entity but we live in different places ... yet we're the same! They say I've got some kind of psychological problem and they insist we are all different, individual people.

They are right, kind of. We are not linked in a psychic way like some siblings. I've never felt a mysterious pain in my eyebrows, only to later discover that Daisy was getting her threading done by a clumsy beauty therapist fifteen miles away. The closest we got to that was one time when Lilly and I both watched *Good Will Hunting* on the same night, but she was in Cork and I was in Dublin. We were both wondering, simultaneously, how Minnie Driver got her hair so straight. Spooky!

We can't read each other's minds, we do usually know what each other is thinking, if you get me. We were all surprised in June of last year – shocked, actually – when my sister Rosie came home with her nails painted a sort of taupe colour. She's always favoured corals and fuchsias. As we gathered around and looked at her with concern, she couldn't explain why she'd switched it up. She just kept saying the nail technician talked her into it and reassured us that she'd go back to the pinks the next time.

We have a lot in common, us Higgins sisters. If our lives together were a sitcom, we'd fall for the same man. That has yet to happen. We are careful to spread the love around to many different men. Not that many. Not in a bad way. Just a normal number, I think. But then, it's hard to know how many is normal, isn't it? Anyway, I'll go and do a count and get back to you ... I may be some time.

Let's get specific. What we have in common is as follows. We wear black eyeliner whenever possible. Children automatically like us. We love Beyoncé. And, in a mean way, we all find potpourri hilariously dated and try-hard. When we leave a house containing even a trace of perfumed plant material, one of us inevitably says something like: *Did you see on top of the bathroom cabinet?* Then we all laugh, cruelly. This is exclusively a sister thing. Our father, for example, is not in this loop. He is a kind man whose hobby is measuring distances with his feet, not judging people. His favourite thing in the world is when the family are all together. He talks about it wistfully, as if it rarely happens.

Oh, imagine if Oliver made it home for Easter and we could all sit around the table – wouldn't that be lovely?

We say: *Like last weekend, you mean, Daddy?*

And he goes into a dream-like state. *Yes, exactly, wasn't that just fabulous? To have ye all here.*

When I was in Edinburgh for the Fringe Festival last year, a selection of my sisters came to stay for a few days. This pleased my father no end – he phoned me a number of times to get among the excitement himself. *Well, what time is their flight? Did you check the smoke alarms in your apartment? Are you all ready for them?*

I raised my eyes to heaven and said: *Yes Daddy, I'm ready for them. I have numerous bowls of potpourri dotted around the place.* I emphasised the word 'numerous' to show how great at sarcasm I am.

To which he replied: *Oh yum. Lovely, they'll be starving. Well done, love.*

Ouch! That made my heart wince. Not only did he not know to laugh at potpourri, he didn't even know what it was. He thought it was a snack laid on by a loving sister. That's how far away he is from the monsters he helped create.

I don't feel too bad about it, though: we are different to our father because of our ages and life experience. As a child, he drank unpasteurised milk, never saw a computer and wasn't encouraged to talk about his feelings. I collected eggs and wore homemade clothes as a child too – but I also ate couscous and was listened to, and that has made all the difference. I suppose future Higginses will be different again – they'll take food in tablet form and wear silver outfits and blue wigs, and communicate their emotions to search engines in ones and zeroes.

Some of my sisters now have children of their own. I can't help suspecting that their loyalty to us, the original set, is compromised by these lovable new imposters. I fear that if my sister Lilly had to choose between, say, watching her son take his first steps and watching me try on jeans, she'd choose the toddling. Even though she knows how hard it is for me to find jeans. I suppose one day, when I'm much older, I'll choose a mate and multiply with them too. Then I'll see what it's like to have divided loyalties of my own.

For the past four years, I've lived with my sister Raedi. My favourite thing in the world is to stand behind something and eavesdrop, as she introduces herself to someone. She has to say her name about twenty-three times, and I like how patient she is about it. Nobody can ever spell her name – she gave it to herself as a three-year-old, and it stuck. Raedi is four years younger than me, but has taken to the role of my carer with a dignity befitting someone much older. She won't even admit that's what she is, but she quietly makes sure there are vegetables in the house, and that I remain socialised to an acceptable level.

If I'm not sure what to do in any given situation -- from deciding what time to go to bed at right up to who to go to bed with – I simply look at my tattoo, asking: *What would Radie [sic] do?* (The tattoo's in Tibetan and streaks right across my abdomen.) Then, I know: 10.30 p.m. at the latest, and definitely not the guy who talked through songs at an open mic night, then clapped loudly like the phoney he was.

Sometimes, I worry that I am too big a responsibility for a young girl and I ask Raedi how she is finding it. That conversation usually goes like this:

Me: *We have a good time, don't we?*

Raedi: *Maeve, stop going on about that.*

My friend's child, a cutie named Kai, asked me recently if Raedi was my partner. I was taken aback, but I know a trick. Children often talk about things they don't understand, so you must ask what they mean before you give the game away. More often than not, they don't even understand what they're on about and you can then skate around the subject. I asked Kai what he meant by 'partner'. He said: *You know, like, you cook together and you sleep together and you live together.*

I tell him that I do live with Raedi, but I do *not* cook with her. The only way in which I cook with her is to hover nearby as she puts the finishing touches to a dish, and plead with her not to slip Tuesday's shrivelled pasta into the lamb curry. She has inherited our mother's 'waste not, want not' compulsion to use tiny scraps of leftovers to ruin brand new meals. It's unbearable to witness and brings out the worst in me. She can't help herself, and I jeer from the sidelines: *Oh great, yes please – why not pop that tablespoon of coconut milk you saved from last week's soup into the meatballs – why don't you, Raedi? Shame to let it go to waste – there's just enough to make the beef taste like sun cream.*

There has been a host of bestsellers written about depressing childhoods: books like *My Auntie Swapped Me for a Jar of Pesto* and *I Hate You, Limerick* have been snapped up by eager readers. I am adding to that legacy with the following bleak memory. That is, of 'Fridge-Tidy-Fridays'. These were the words my mother would sing out, as she called us for this grim and most surprising of meals. We would approach the table with trepidation, our eyes scanning over the dozens of miniature helpings of foodstuffs. Unwanted portions of the week gone by lingered there, resurrected for one last stand and ready to meet their makers. An egg cup of rice pudding; an upturned button holding a microscopic cube of wizened lasagne; a solitary pineapple ring with a gap in it.

Unsurprising, considering my mother gets multiple uses from a single sheet of aluminium foil. After it's protected a hundred roast chickens from getting burnt, she passes it on to the school for use in the construction of angel wings or donates it to the local heroin user. My mother simply cannot bear waste. She hoards slivers of soap under the sink for years, until she has the required number – a number only she knows – to create a grotesque Frankenstein's monster of soap leftovers, which hulks on the sink, daring us to find a way of using it.

Now, when Raedi is going to the supermarket, I insist she gets soap in a pump-action dispenser. She does the grocery shopping because she has a car and she can drive. Another reason I leave it up to her is that I get distracted by special offers and shiny packaging and often return home with a hundred sausages, some glittering teacakes and no change. So we have a system where Raedi does the shopping and I make requests, like for the pump-action soap dispensers. They are better than bars of soap, because you don't rub germs all over them, they don't need a slimy saucer to sit in and, most importantly, because they show visitors how far up the ladder of richness we've come. Although nobody has ever commented on how I have exclusively pump-action soap in my house, because the people who notice such things are themselves the epitome of discretion and class.

As for the other item on Kai's partner agenda – sleeping together – it's simply not the case. Raedi and I do live together and we do go to bed at around the same time, but we sleep in separate rooms. We are like an elderly couple who've long ceased all physical contact but remain great friends. It's about the companionship, really, the shared history, and like I said, it's so handy for grocery shopping. I do sometimes want to go into her room to wake her up and tell her something, but she has drawn the line at such neediness and banned me from doing so, except in emergencies. She made that rule after I couldn't help waking her one night to relay how I'd been on the tram and the ticket inspectors came on and for about three minutes I couldn't find my ticket – but then I found it.

I sometimes tell her she should leave me. She's young and has her whole life ahead of her. She looks hopeful when I start saying that, but then trouble clouds her face and she says that before she can consider it, I must learn how to drive, I must stop crying when I see old men combing their hair on the bus, and I have to remember to eat my greens, every day.

That pickled onion hit
I love so much

People cry 'stalker' too lightly. You bump into them at a market stall and have a chat about how carrots really do taste better when you know what the farmer's kids look like. Forty-five minutes later, you stand behind them in line for a falafel and they scream: *Oh my God, I'm your stalker! Everywhere you go, there I am! Hahaha!* I don't laugh. I explain to them that because we are the same basic type of person – the type of person who listens to earnest radio documentaries and aspires to learn more about keeping bees in urban areas – so we are bound to come across each other most days in a city the size of Dublin. I also tell them that seeing them at a book launch, then in a bakery in the same afternoon is very different to being stalked by them – and that I should know. At this point, I look into the middle distance and I sweep off. I leave them with a bit of mystery, in that grand tradition of women in my family: we love to hint darkly at something bad that may or may not have befallen us, and leave it at that.

I can never fully leave things at that, though, so I will tell you all about it. I want this to be like a slumber party. It's already late but there's so much to talk about. So you must lie, tummy-down on the bed, prop up on your elbows and cup your face with your little hands. In other words: prepare for drama!

Ages ago, I went out with a creepy guy for about three weeks. It was super casual and I didn't realise back then that he was creepy. From what I remember, at first he was just kind of weird. He drank a lot and had the shakes and was really jumpy. I know that most ladies love a shell-shocked oddball, but he wasn't for me. I didn't see or hear from him for about six years, until he e-mailed me last year to say a) that he was in love with me and wanted to marry me; b) that there was an international conspiracy of arms dealers trying to ruin his reputation; and c) that he was absolutely not crazy.

I e-mailed him back to thank him for getting in contact but said that I honestly didn't think we should get married. It was stupid of me to reply that one time. What followed were dozens of e-mails from him with the same basic themes: that I was his future wife but didn't seem to realise it; that he just needed to see me to discuss it and everything would be fine. It wasn't scary – like seeing a cat with no eyes or hearing you need root canal treatment – but it was worrying. It seemed like he was not fully with it in the old 'this is real, this is my imagination' department. I made a G-mail folder, labelled it 'Creepy Guy', and had his e-mails go directly there.

I didn't think about it again, until a radio station I some-times work for got in touch to say someone had been sending in requests for me – hundreds of them. He'd also sent gifts for me to the station. Although I have no formal training in detective work, I thought to myself: *This has to be the same creepy guy who is e-mailing me*. It was. I asked my agent for advice. I thought he might know what to do because he's got some big names on his books – for example, Des Bishop. Oh, Dezzi B. Big Boy Bishop. I call him Desmond Tutu, because he's too, too handsome! He certainly is an anomaly – a great-looking comedian. I try and treat him like the rest of the guys (comedians are guys), but it's hard because he's just so handsome. I always want to put lipstick on when he's nearby – I don't know why!! Anyway, about the stalker, my agent told me he didn't come across this kind of thing much, and to go and talk to the police, just to see what they have to say. I said I would leave it a few weeks, but he said to maybe go and talk to them right away.

So I went to my local station, which was under construction at the time. I was embarrassed about going to the police: nothing had actually happened, really. A frozen garda sat in a prefab building, looking hard done by. I promised I wouldn't take up too much time and told him briefly what had been happening. He folded his arms, and looked at me sceptically as I talked.

I heard myself getting more and more apologetic. I think I finished up by saying: *So, I know it's stupid and there's nothing to worry about really – just thought I should mention it to see what you think.*

He picked up his pen and tapped it on the desk three times. Then he said: *So, your ex wants to get back with you, is it?*

I said: *Well, we were never actually going out, it's kind of —* He cut me off by saying: *Look, just give him a ring and tell him it's all over.*

I said: *Oh, I don't have his number.*

To this, he said: *Can you not get it?*

At this point I think the slumber party is going great, don't you? You're dying to hear whether or not I took the garda's advice about opening up a new channel of communication with the creepy guy. I will tell you, but first let's go to the toilet then have some peanut M&Ms ...

OK, so, I didn't take the garda's advice but I did feel kind of mortified. I was worried I'd made a big deal out of a situation that didn't even qualify as stalking. Most stalkers are diligent and show up absolutely everywhere their victim is. As opposed to tracking me down, the creepy guy would often just e-mail and tell me where he would be on a given afternoon, and request that I come and meet him there. And he would not give me much notice. I suppose I was lucky that my 'stalker' was disorganised and, I guessed, regularly hospitalised.

I was beginning to doubt his commitment, until he suddenly got it together and began showing up at my gigs, albeit just the heavily publicised ones. He waited outside after one, and before I could get away, he talked to me directly. He didn't threaten me or anything: it was just unnerving because I hadn't seen him in years and now he was bothering me and being wild-eyed and illogical, like a classic dangerous person from a cartoon. At that point, I decided to give the po-po another go.

This time I was prepared. I printed the weirdest of the e-mails and brought them with me. I learned off the most relevant murder statistics. The radio station printed off some of the text messages he'd sent about me – at this stage, in their thousands. The creepy guy would later tell the police that he thought I was communicating with him through the music played on the radio. As if even the combined might of Maroon 5 and Flo Rida could have adequately conveyed the only message I was sending, which was, of course: *LEAVE ME ALONE!*

I didn't go back to my local Garda station – instead I went to one in the city centre, in the hope of a more enlightened response. My heart sank when I caught a glimpse of the officer on duty through the window: he was leaning into an office chair with his hands behind his head, legs wide apart, feet planted on the floor – classic alpha male pose. I assumed he would brush me off, so when he came out to the desk, I told him about the creepy guy as sternly as I could.

Whenever I am trying to be serious, people recognise me from TV and don't believe me – this is my cosmic punishment for taking part in a hidden camera show. The garda recognised me but didn't ask if I was up to my old pranking tricks. He was professional. He was also totally handsome, not like the garda the last time, who was not even 10 per cent handsome. (I don't mean to objectify these men: I'm just trying to paint a picture for you with my words.)

He read over some of the e-mails, asked some questions, and then said, gesturing to my helmet on the desk: *I see you cycled here.* I said I had, and for a moment thought he might ask to see my lights. Instead he said: *Well, before you get back on your bike, you should check and see that it's not been interfered with.* That had never crossed my mind. What could the creepy guy do? Put streamers on the handles to make me more identifiable? Loosen the brakes? Maybe. I was pleased the garda was taking me seriously, but his concern made a dull dread – one that had been shadowing me since the whole thing started – settle itself heavily on top of my shoulders.

He said he'd talk to his superiors about what to do next, and told me to come back and make a statement the following day. I left and checked my bike carefully. Nothing was different except for an empty Meanies bag someone had thrown into the basket. I ran my finger around the inside of it, and got that pickled onion hit I love so much, then cycled home. When I went back to the station the next day, the garda showed me into a little room and gave me a glass of water. I know – what a total flirt!

Anyway, he asked if I could hear voices from the room next door. I listened for a moment and could hear some muffled chatting. He said: *They're some bank robbers we picked up earlier, but they're well locked up, so you're safe.* He actually said 'bank robbers' and if my memory serves me, he may also have flexed. He then asked me lots of questions and noted down my answers in careful blue biro.

All of this good work however was undermined by the distracting fact that he could not stop burping. He would try and say something, then his throat would make a gurgling noise and he'd cover his mouth, and either hiccup or belch. It was sort of gross but fascinating, and made more so by him pretending it wasn't happening. After about ten minutes of eruptions, I told him I could come back another day if he wasn't feeling well. He insisted that he was fine, kind of shouting the 'ine' part of 'fine' with a particularly aggressive belch. Then he looked down at the ground and, between rumblings, explained that just before I'd arrived, the other gardai had dared him to swallow a couple of Berocca. You know – those effervescent vitamin tablets you're supposed to dilute in water.

The fizzing subsided after about twenty minutes, and we finished up the statement. Then I noticed I had six missed calls from a booker and suddenly remembered I was supposed to be on stage in ten minutes. I had forgotten about my spot at a city-centre comedy night for drunks and tourists. I told the garda and he said he'd drop me down. I protested for about half a second but followed him out to the corridor, where he yelled that he needed a car – fast. Someone threw him a set of keys which he leapt to catch, and we raced out and jumped into one of a number of Honda Civics. We sped along city streets and through amber lights. For a brief moment, I was Cagney and he was Lacey, but much hotter. I made it to the show on time, and totally pumped. The host called my name, and I took to the stage. A red-faced man snoozed gently in the front row and eleven Norwegians looked on impassively, as I breathlessly relived what had just happened.

In the end, the burping hero arrested the creepy guy and told him to stop contacting the princess of comedy. That did the trick. I got a few more e-mails, apologising, saying he'd been diagnosed with a mental illness but was feeling better and would be in Bewley's on Grafton Street between 4 p.m. and 5 p.m., if I felt popping in. I didn't. After that, he stopped hassling me.

Ideally, I would prefer if the whole thing never happened. That said, I did get a spin in an unmarked car, I did meet Ireland's dreamiest garda *and* I got his number. For emergencies only – but still, how do you like them apples?!

Also, talk about life imitating art! For a few months I practically became Whitney Houston's character in what could basically be my biopic, *The Bodyguard*.

There are, however, some fundamental differences between Rachel Marron's and my story. I'll list them for you:

1. Rachel's sister Nicki was behind the whole thing: she took out a contract on Rachel's life. I've got to be honest. For a time, I did suspect that my sister Raedi was the puppet master. Like Nicki, Raedi has a big dog, Raedi lives with her superstar sister, and Raedi has no public profile. She has never expressed an interest in being on stage, but who doesn't want my life? So I tested Raedi. I'd tell her what was going on: *So, the creepy guy showed up at my gig today and sent me a dozen more e-mails*

   Then I'd watch closely for any flicker of 'job well done' in her eyes. All I saw was growing concern. I checked her phone for text messages to hit men. I was on the alert for messages like: *Target jus buyin after8s in Eurospar, kill now xx Raedi* – but I just found ones about running. (That girl is obsessed with running, as are her friends.) All the messages were, like: *Do u like runnin? I luv it* and *Let's go runnin l8er* and *OK ;-)*. No mention of assassination. Finally I realised and accepted that if Raedi wanted me dead, she could kill me herself, simply by not doing the food shopping one week, or by hiding my quilt.

2. In the film, Rachel Marron is surrounded by people
    all the time, but I'm usually either on my own or
    with one or maybe two people. Lots of the people
    around her work for her: I don't have any employees.
    If I did, I'd have better ones than she does. Tony, for
    example – that lumpen bozo of a security guard – is
    clearly underperforming. He's always snacking and
    not noticing that the camera wires have been cut.
    Her PR man is called Sy and is extremely bitchy. The
    PR people I know are serious and pleasant ladies,
    usually with blonde hair, who encourage me to be
    less down on myself in interviews.

    They don't organise pop-up appearances in
    nightclubs, where I get to wear a tin foil helmet and
    be the Queen of the Night. Instead, they spend a
    lot of time wringing their hands in hotel lobbies,
    while I refuse to peep out from between two sofa
    cushions for some boneheaded photographer.
    Later in the film, in the messy aftermath of the
    assassination attempt at the Oscars ceremony, we
    see Sy quietly retrieve the card with the winner's
    name written on it. He wipes some blood off and
    pockets it, and this really drives home to us just
    where his priorities lie.

3. Rachel gets nominated for an Oscar. I have never
    been nominated for an Oscar. However, as you all
    know, the hidden camera show I was in did win an
    IFTA in, I believe, 2007, or else 2008. An IFTA is
    exactly like an Oscar, when you think about it.

4. Rachel has a 'show' bedroom that she uses for photo shoots; she also has a normal bedroom for sleeping in and leaving her dirty washing on the floor. I just have the one bedroom. She also has a separate kitchen and living area, while my kitchen and living area are open-plan. I'd prefer her house. In one scene, Kevin Costner is trying to have a sandwich, when Tony, that dopey lug, starts on him and they have a fist-fight. Pots and pans go flying and crockery gets smashed, but it doesn't seem to disturb the rest of the household. That's the beauty of separate rooms.

5. Rachel is immaculately turned out, always. She has amazing clothes: capes and gowns and glittering bustiers. When she's going jogging, she has a special outfit with a matching headband. When she is practising her dancing, she has a cool leotard. Even in one scene where she has a hangover, she is wearing a lovely robe and her hair is perfect.

    All of that is in sharp relief to what I was wearing, say, earlier today. I cycled home from the gym, so had one leg of my tracksuit pants rolled up. I left it like that. The dog had got hold of some onions and ripped them up all over the kitchen/living room, so I had to wash the floor. I did so in my socks, to avoid leaving prints. Then I went to get the post but didn't bother putting my shoes back on, instead I wedged my red flip-flops on over my socks. It was chilly out, so I completed the 'Is

she OK?' look by putting on my relaxing jumper,
which is huge and grey and covered in music notes.

So, these are the main points of contrast between myself and Rachel from *The Bodyguard*. Everything else that happened is pretty much the same, particularly the end of our sagas. Just yesterday, I was getting on my private jet in my good headscarf. I was sort of bummed out, because my new bodyguard is a real fuddy-duddy, with white hair and a moustache. Then I looked out the window, and who did I see? You guessed it – The Bodygarda!! (sorry). His arm in a sling and everything. You know the rest. We are very happy. Now, it is after getting very late. No. More. Talking. We'd better brush our teeth and go to sleep!

You want the beautiful fairy to hold the cake away from the big fat monster?

As a do-gooder, I really must do better. My status as a major hotshot in the world of Irish entertainment means a number of organisations and charities tend to ask me to help them out in various ways. I have a chronic inability to say no, as well as a rabid ego, so I often do as they ask. Not always, though. Here are some requests for help that I have managed to turn down:

- Organising a fundraising show for a nineteen-year-old who had taken out a credit union loan to go to America on a J-1, then broke his arm and couldn't work over there. All he could do was go drinking on the beach, so he couldn't really pay back the loan and the credit union weren't being sound about it.

- Being quizmaster at a table quiz to raise money for a Navan-based frisbee team hoping to, in their own words, *set up some kind of tournament next summer*.

– Doing a photo shoot with my cat to be made into Christmas cards for an animal charity. I did want to do this one, but I knew Little Edie wouldn't co-operate. I was also unconvinced as to who would buy the cards, but you know men – they're into all sorts of images.

And here are some ventures I've agreed to help out with, Mother Teresa style:

1. A photo shoot held at the zoo for a hospital fundraiser

I arrived a few minutes late and rushed into the café where I was to meet the photographer, people from the fundraising team and the other people who were going to be in the photos. These other people are often some of the beneficiaries of the charity, or on occasion GAA players or musicians. Frequently, however, they are models. In this case, there was a model dressed as Cinderella and three children from the hospital dressed as sort of pirate-koala-princesses. I didn't realise we were supposed to be in costume, and I said this to the PR woman who was organising the shoot. She said that of course I didn't have to wear a costume, but asked if I could possibly paint the children's faces? She said she would herself, only she was concerned she might disturb one of their feeding tubes. So I did a great and careful job with the face-painting and we all headed out to the hippos.

The model and the children played a blinder: they giggled and grinned for the camera, pointed at monkeys and looked adorable. Nobody asked me to be in the photos, though the photographer did ask me to hold one of his lights. A woman wearing a T-shirt with a cartoon child on crutches on the back gestured to one of the children and asked me under her breath: *How is that little one doing?* I didn't know why she was asking me and didn't appreciate her gossipy tone, but I replied as best I could: *I don't know – she looks kind of mustard, but that could be a positive sign.*

She backed away. I realised that everybody thought I was a nurse. I should have known – it happens a lot. Deep in my heart, I know that I look like a nurse. I have an open, helpful face, prone to redness. I have grand, wide hips and curly hair. There is a faint whiff of martyr off me. All I'm missing is a hint of capability. I knew I should speak up about my real identity as a big-time showbiz star, but it was too late in the day. Eventually, as I traipsed along behind the group, holding discarded coats and a stepladder, the PR woman asked me – very nicely but very directly – who I was. I said I was a comedian called Maeve and had been asked to come along to get some photos taken to publicise the fundraiser.

She shook her head, looked at me hard and consulted her Blackberry. Suddenly it was like she saw me for the first time: *You're the comedian girl? Maeve! Wonderful. Well, I'm thrilled you could make it! This will really help the event's profile!* And so, for the last few minutes of the shoot, Cinderella and the kids were shunted out of the way and all the adults made a big fuss of me. The ladder I'd been carrying was spirited away. I was handed a hairband with koala ears on it and a magic wand. Someone even offered

me a Jelly Baby. *That's great, Mary – good job!* shouted the photographer, enthusiastically snapping as I posed in front of the reptile house. The PR woman hissed at him: *It's not Mary, it's Maeve.* Then, to nobody in particular, she added: *And we're very lucky to have her.*

2. Attend the launch of a healthy-eating cookbook in aid of a charity

This one seemed quite straightforward. I had to show up, say well done to everyone on making this book and get my picture taken with a copy of said book. The location was a city-centre park on an incredibly windy day. I arrived just in time to see a model in a tiny dress chasing after one of her hair extensions, which had been blown off by a gust of wind. I didn't realise there was going to be a model and considered running away. The PR lady saw the look on my face and explained that using a model for the shoot was their only hope of getting into some of the papers and Amber was very popular. Amber did seem lovely, but of course, that wasn't the point.

When the photographer handed Amber a huge cream cake and told me to act like I wanted to take it off her, I objected: *You want the beautiful fairy to hold the cake away from the big fat monster?*

The PR lady stepped in, laughing lightly: *Oh that's awful, don't be so hard on yourself! Now, if you could kind of lunge towards her for a second, it'll make a great shot. Amber – look scared! Exaggerate now girls, come on!*

3. Turning on the Christmas lights in Cork city

This was the best day of my life. My parents were really proud of me and I got free cake and sausages from the stallholders in the English Market. Someone from the council had made a huge lever like the one you push in cartoons, and I battled the Mayor out of the way to push it down. There was a choir of ancient men on stage singing Christmas carols, and there were also puppies. Everyone cheered and the lights were gorgeous.

Could you just try and smile at the beans?

It's easy to tell who's cool. Runners with their hoods up, cyclists with their arms folded, fathers who don't smoke: they are all cool. If you're cool, you just know you are and you don't have to think about it – you just tuck your shirt into your jeans and live your life. If you ask yourself whether or not you're cool, that means – automatically – that you're not cool.

Knowing whether or not you're famous is a different story. Becoming famous in Ireland is easily achieved: you just have to fall on some ice or be an insistent accountant, and you'll find yourself on television. Most people watch television, and they will recognise you from that – but not always from that. Often, a person looks at me quizzically and asks where they know me from. I learned the hard way not to say: *Probably from your TV screen, babe,* because they're usually just mistaking me for one of my Waterford cousins.

And it's unsettling to have to recite an ever-more obscure list of TV appearances to strangers, as they try and put two and two together. The last time I voted, I had to give my name to the registrar to get my ballot paper. She looked at me long and hard, and said: *You seem familiar – how do I know you?* I asked if she was from Waterford and if she knew the Walshes. She said she wasn't, and she didn't. I asked her if she watched hidden-camera shows – she said she did not and that they are desperate things altogether. I suggested that maybe she saw me on a chat show, and that seemed to ignite some outrage on her part: *I barely watch television! Sure, when would I have time to watch television?* She enlisted the help of a motorbike courier who was putting on his leathers behind a screen nearby: *Patrick, who is this girl?*

Patrick walked around to face me, looked me up and down, and said: *I haven't a clue. What's her name?* I felt like one of those perfectly 'with-it' disabled ladies whose husbands get asked if they take sugar.

Higgins, said the registrar. *Maeve Higgins.* They both shook their heads and the courier zipped up his jacket and wandered off. She muttered to herself: *Very familiar. That's annoying me now. Anyway, it'll come to me.* Then she said to me: *Come on, here's your slip – there's a queue of people behind you!*

I never consciously wanted to be famous – and I'm not famous, just kind of well known. This is the level I am at: if I were a cleaning product, I'd be an ecological alternative to a household name – one that people are vaguely familiar with, but wouldn't necessarily include in their weekly shop. I don't want to be too down on myself, though – there are certainly times when being recognised helps me up in this crazy old world. For example, I once got upgraded in a Limerick hotel by a receptionist who happened to be a fan. I was sent up to the penthouse, the honeymoon suite. It was five rooms and hadn't been occupied in a long time – I could tell by the way the cowhide recliner creaked when I reclined into it. There was a full dining room with twelve wine glasses and a microwave. I was a regular Little Lord Fauntleroy that night, living it up with a giant bed all to myself, looking out at the grey November river from my wraparound balcony.

Another time my star currency came into play was when I got an eye infection. A nurse who liked my TV show *Fancy Vittles* let me skip the queue, proving that I made the right decision to stop paying for private health insurance after all, *Mammy*.

I was in a hidden camera show for a few years. It wasn't very mean-spirited, but I do feel sheepish if I happen to see some of the people we wound up. And I see them all the time, because Dublin is small and I cycle around a lot. The show, *Naked Camera*, made me recognisable to a select group of people – for example, gardai always recognise me from it, as do people who have been in prison. I was told, by a former inmate of Mountjoy Gaol, that *Naked Camera* was big on the inside. In the Venn diagram of the life experience of a garda and a prisoner, hidden-camera shows and court appearances are both in the intersection. I imagine that carvery and porn are also in there, but cannot be sure.

I recently found myself in urgent need of fennel and human contact, so I took a trip to town. At the bus stop, two women in matching tracksuits shared a cigarette and dominated proceedings. There was about three years between them, and they looked very alike. I guessed they were either sisters or mother and daughter. The older one was loudly instructing the younger one to trade in her earrings at a Cash-4-Gold in order to get money for that night's drinking. She added (unkindly, I felt): *They're real ugly things in anyways.* The younger one looked downcast and her hand self-consciously went up to her gold hoops. Both women were then silent for a while, and then I felt them staring at my face. I pretended to text, the non-wizard's version of an invisibility cloak. It didn't work. The older one said loudly: *Ah, look at the state of your one's phone, and she thinks she's real famous and all. Sap!*

Everyone not wearing headphones at the bus stop turned to look at me. I held up my little phone as if it was a prize on a game show. I thought this was a great move, but it angered the lady: *Ah, she thinks she's so great, but she's still getting the bus like any other dope. Fuck's sake.* I wanted to defend myself and tell her not to be such a Thatcherite, but I was nervous that she'd scratch or bite me, so I remained silent. Luckily, an old lady with lipstick all over her face came along and the two busied themselves jeering at her, so I was off the hook.

Usually, people are nicer about recognising me than the woman in a tracksuit was. Sometimes people look at me, then look away with a funny smile on their faces, like they know a secret. I want to say to them: *I beg your pardon, but you don't have a secret. I too realise that I am – intermittently and with varying levels of success – on Irish TV some weekday evenings.*

People won't recognise you when you're trying to get a table in a busy restaurant, but they will spot you with toothpaste stains all down your T-shirt, as you finger curtain remnants in your local charity shop. Nobody will whisper your name reverently and whisk you backstage to meet Bruce Springsteen – but they'll definitely clock who you are as you pick at your face absentmindedly in the reflection of a car window you thought was unoccupied.

Yoga teachers never have a clue who I am, neither do teenage boys. Girls in flowery dresses and middle-aged gay men usually do, however. These are my favourites. They approach me in vegetarian restaurants and apologise for bothering me. I tell them they're not bothering me, and they blush and say they loved the show. I say thanks so much, and they blush harder and go back to their quinoa salad. I resist the urge to scoop them up and keep them in my attic for hugs. It's tricky to know what to say when a stranger compliments your work. As with so many things – marriage proposals, offers of a kitten, a child handing you a grotesque crayon drawing of you as a bee – the best thing to do is smile and say thank you.

That's easier said than done, though. I tend to go overboard when flattered. Last summer, an American lady came and talked to me after a show I'd just done in Dublin. She said she had arranged her holiday around seeing my show. I was so taken aback, and had a tedious 'just-for-little-old-me?' moment. I immediately began apologising to her. I told her I regretted having had a Bounty bar before the show as it had made me giddy for the first half and sleepy for the second. She was so nice about it, and said she hadn't even noticed. I suggested some other comedians she should go and see. She said I was her favourite and she wasn't interested in seeing other shows. I was so brimful of slavering gratitude that I grabbed her arm, and said we should go for lunch. She physically stepped back and said she was just saying hello and that she was on holiday with her *husband*. Hot damn! She assumed I was a sleazy comedian who hits on the audience after the show. Not me, lady! I can't even make eye contact with the audience after a show, because I've just told them things I didn't even realise I was feeling.

Most of us comedians start out in life as ugly monsters on society's fringes, until we discover a minor super-power: the ability to make strangers laugh. Through this, we attain some fame and money. We then begin to use that power for bad, doing things like sleeping with starstruck youngsters for fun, and making crummy TV shows for money. What a pack of naughty dogs we can be! You have to watch out for us – especially if you're a nineteen-year-old girl in a skirt sitting near the front.

Not all of us are like this, of course – some, anchored by a wife or ethics or timidity, figure out how to be decent citizens and do minimal damage to the world. I hope I'm somewhere in the middle. I've never taken advantage of what's rottenly known as a 'gag-hag' (granted, it's tricky for me to do so, being a straight woman), but I have guiltily pitched some god-awful ideas for TV shows, in the dual hope they will not be watched but I will be paid some development money. I have yet to actually be in something I'm ashamed of. But there's plenty time yet.

When I first started working in TV, I got asked to be in quite a few ads. I turned them all down because I didn't want to be a sellout: a charming notion I picked up from the 1960s. That's the truth, but not the whole truth. The type of ads I got asked to do also had a bearing on my turning them down. They were – exclusively – ads for boring food, with a funny bit at the end.

In one heady week in 2007, not one, but *two* baked bean manufacturers wanted my services. Here is an approximation of the proposed scripts:

Brandname Bean Advert No. 1

INTERIOR : Kitchen with a retro vibe (gingham curtains, willow-pattern china).

MOTHER (a happy, chubby woman with curly hair) spoons beans from a silver saucepan onto the waiting plates of toast held by her children (two happy, chubby children with curly hair).

CUT TO: The family dog (a happy, chubby dog with curly hair) jumps onto chair and noses a plate towards the mother. The dog is trying to get a serving of baked beans! *Mother shakes her head but smiles; children laugh; the dog puts its head to one side.*

Ends on close-up of beans.

Brandname Bean Advert No. 2

INTERIOR : Kitchen in the style of the 1950s (teapot, oilskin tablecloth).

MOTHER (a portly, smiling woman with wavy hair) spoons beans from a silver saucepan onto her husband's plate of buttered toast. Father (a portly, smiling man with a slight kink in his hair) swaps seats and holds up a second clean plate. The father is trying to get a double serving of baked beans. All laugh wholeheartedly.

Ends on close-up of beans.

I can read the scriptwriters' minds. They were thinking: *We need someone to sell beans on toast. That Higgins girl can do nourishing, self-sacrificing, reliable and kind of funny, right?* Right. But that doesn't make it right! Why don't they just come clean, and put out a casting call out for the plainest girl in Ireland? Why don't they say to my face: *Maeve, you seem to us like the kind of woman who'd put up with a cheating husband as long as he agreed to have a shower afterwards and not mention the other women in front of the kids.*

I have never been approached about doing any innuendo-based ads. You know, ones where a guy seasons a raw chicken, then suddenly an attractive woman leaps on him from the kitchen cabinet and the tagline is something like: *If you get chicken ... you'll get sex.* Why not? I could do sexy! I can be smokin', believe me. At the moment I'm wearing a velour tracksuit pantsuit that is too small for me – but that's only because there are no cameras or hot guys around. For all the ad men know, I could be great at draping myself across a chaise longue in a cheap dress, talking in a charged way about what a bargain this particular forty-inch TV is.

I wonder what would happen if I woke up one morning and realised I'd become one of those desperadoes who endorses any old product on TV? I like to think I'd have a bowl of Sugar Puffs and kill myself. I know it's not cool to joke about that, because there's gluten in Sugar Puffs and I'm intolerant – but that just goes to show you how principled I am.

One of these days, I may well fall from up-here-on-my-high-horse. Until then, I will continue to squint down in judgment. The reason I'm squinting is that I have extremely light-sensitive eyes but I'm afraid to wear sunglasses. You see, I'm worried that people might think I'm wearing them in a celebrity-in-disguise way, and come to the conclusion that I've got ideas above my station. So I don't wear sunglasses. It's an exquisite punishment I dole out to myself on sunny days.

Switch it up: career ideas for the adaptable lady

Mistaken-For Job

A maitre d' in a restaurant recently did a double take as he refused me a table, and said he thought he knew me from somewhere. I have a stock response to people who say that. *Your dreams?* I ask – then do a little laugh. *Aren't I funny?* But this guy said, quite seriously: *No. Are you a dancer?* Thereby making my day. I know it's his job to make me feel good about not getting the booth I wanted, but I don't care. Me, a dancer? I can see that. I float about from place to place; I am graceful and easily frightened. I wear loose cotton clothes that hang off my shoulders. My dainty ankles are stronger than they look. I am a dancer! Tap, modern, ballet: these are all languages to me. I move my lithe body about, to communicate how I'm feeling – which is never hungry. I perch. I flit. I stretch all of the time. I wear headbands but a perfect auburn lock always escapes. I don't sweat but after rehearsal, I am flushed and dewy. I put on a wrap cardigan, and sip herbal tea as I concentrate on the choreographer's instructions. After a twenty-minute pause, I come to and tell him: *Yes, I am a dancer*.

Dream Job

I think I would be a good prison governor. I'm tough, but fair. I believe there's some good in everyone. I like to help a fellow up. I would be loved and respected by the prisoners. *She's alright*, the grizzly old-timers would growl to the fresh meat as I swish past. *You don't mess with her, and she don't mess with you.*

I'd start a music programme in the jail, and they could learn the oboe and channel their frustrations that way. If the jail I am assigned to already has a music programme, I would cancel it and start some other project that rehabilitates criminals' hearts as well as their minds. For example, I would give them each a little terrier and they could train it to do tasks for others – like running along the shoulders of the elderly, as a light massage. I would also work on the physical fitness of the prisoners. I would introduce quality protein to their diets and make them bench press their own bodyweight and do chins every morning, so they would get incredibly ripped. That way, their self-esteem would improve and Momma would have something pretty to look at. My Victorian ideals and outdated notions would make me a cool, retro-style prison governor, I'm sure of it.

Using My Talents Job

I don't think I'm exactly psychic but I do have a chilling habit of guessing the exact situation that is upsetting a person and referring to it in a jokey way, thereby setting them off. My top three gaffes of 2012 so far are:

1. And is that when your Dad ran off?

2. I guess that's what happens when you've got an eating disorder!

3. Doesn't touring make you so lonely, you just want to die?

This gift is unhelpful at parties, and has led to me apologising to and comforting people I've just met – but it could potentially become a new revenue path. I could do psychic predictions over the phone; that way I could sort out the plastics drawer, fold the washing and get all my other quiet household chores done as I talk.

Nightmare Job

I would hate to work as a prostitute. I think everybody would, really. Men who pay for sex sometimes justify doing so by saying the woman has made a choice and she should be allowed to do what she wants. Those men are clowning, for real. As if she woke up that morning and thought, *Mmmm, you know what I would love?* As if gender inequality, social marginalisation and possibly being the victim of sex trafficking are irrelevant factors in the woman's decision to give cretins like them a blow job.

The other excuse people use to make them feel OK about prostitution is to insist it's 'the oldest profession in the world'. First of all, I doubt that. What about all those guys who worked as hunters? And haven't people quietly been selling bits and pieces on Ebay for absolutely years at this stage?

Second of all, just because something has been around for ages doesn't mean it's acceptable. If I have a big cotton field and am short on time, I can't steal a family from Kenya and make them pick it for free. It would be handy for me, yes, but it's just not cool to do that anymore. The Kenyans would kick up a fuss and my only comeback would be to weakly berate them for having no sense of tradition.

I think it should be a criminal offence to pay for sex, and that would surely lead to all sorts of mix-ups if I did work as a prostitute. The only position I could do, in good conscience, would be the citizen's arrest. Instead of fake moans, I'd just come right out with the genuine handcuffs and say: *Don't think you can exploit me so blithely, John. You're under arrest!* (Customers are called John, you see. Toilets are also called John. And brazen upstarts who swan into meetings half way through and start bossing people around are known as johnny-come-latelys. And remember how naughty little John McEnroe used to curse and throw his racket down? Johns are nasty pieces of work, I'm telling you.)

Another reason I'd be bad at working as a prostitute is that I hate discussing money. When it comes to splitting the bill in restaurants, I can't bear the long pause that comes with working out who had what, so I usually end up paying for everyone. I'd imagine it would be even more awkward when it came to accepting cash for sex services rendered. I know I'd end up screaming: *No, no, you put your money away now. I'll get this one! Sure, aren't we in your car? Look, I'll get this and you can get the next one.*

My Brother's Job

Oliver is a geologist. Our friend Fifi once made him a T-shirt saying *Geology Rocks*, and he wore it quite a lot, but not in the office. That's the thing – he works out of an office sometimes, and other times on site, where the rocks are. I would be fine in the office situation. I've never worked in one before, but I know the drill, because many of my friends work in offices and I quiz them relentlessly about what happens therein.

Within the office, here's how I would play it. I would pick some friends and some enemies. This staves off boredom. Each week someone would bake a cake to share around the office and, although everyone's always talking about how they need to lose weight, these baked treats would become increasingly, elaborately more competitive.

To distract my boss from my dearth of rock knowledge I would go online, look up volcanoes and print off cool pictures of them. If it came down to it, I could bust out my one cool fact about geology: coal doesn't play half as big a role in the foundation of diamonds as people say it does. Talking about that would get me through at least a couple of hours.

On site, I would dress the part – that is half the battle in any job (particularly if you work as a riot policeman: cringe for you if you show up to work wearing a pair of colourful Bermudas and a sideways baseball cap and have to start fighting an angry mob!). So, on site, I would wear khaki clothes and a hat with corks hanging down and have a little pickaxe hanging off my tool belt. Oliver said that in his work, he uses a lot of technology – to measure air and gas and things – but I think I would take it back to basics, with rock collecting, rock counting and rock measuring.

******News just in******

To research this piece further, I just spoke to Oliver. Turns out, he's actually a hydrogeologist. This means something to do with water. Like maybe, how to get the water out from under the geology – or something along those lines. Until someone explains the difference between palaeontology, archaeology and geology to me, I cannot help feeling that I would be a terrible geologist, and an even worse hydro-geologist – whatever that is.

Dark monkeys with bright paradise faces

Make-up is silent and odourless. It is all around us. It is make-believe's cousin, and both work quietly to improve our daily lot by lifting us above it for a minute or two each day. Make-up is optimistic and a bit silly, like a dreamy friend from school who has never quite got the hang of adult life. Make-up is not a mask – it doesn't hide things, not really. It's more like an anti-depressant – not changing reality, just softening its edges.

I have no formal training as an investigative journalist and Raedi's puppy has eaten the internet connection, but if my memory serves me right, make-up originated thousands of years ago in New York City. A queen was visiting at the time: a famously plain queen. She was inspecting some soldiers when she suddenly fell – face first, into some mud. The mud covered up a blemish on her nose and some spider veins on her right cheek. Two little leaves clung to her eyelids, making her eyes *POP* with colour. Some berries got squashed against her mouth with the force of the fall, making her look sexy. She was transformed! Someone quickly etched her image and everyone went gaga for her new look. All the commoners emulated the newly beautiful queen by daubing themselves in dirt and debris. This evolved into our modern-day lipstick, powder and paint.

I know you can't see me right now so let me tell you, I am currently wearing a *lot* of make-up. Here's what I did today. I put a light browny beige liquid all over the skin on my face and the parts of my neck that are showing. I put a cream-coloured paste under my eyes to disguise the dark circles. I have a lemony yellow colour on my eyelids to make them match the rest of my face, and I have drawn a pinkish circle around my mouth to make it look generous and less like a little boy's mouth. Finally, I isolated and coated each eyelash in black paint. And now I feel just great! All of these potions and particles have brought me up to a regular human girl standard and I look natural and friendly because of it. Thank you, cosmetic industry!

Bear in mind that my plans for the day include nothing more exciting than sitting down and writing to you nosy parkers, and then bothering my sister Raedi about what to do with my winter clothes. I'm having trouble deciding whether to donate them to charity or burn them. Part of me feels like it's rude to expect people, even poor people, to wear my velour hoody from five years ago with a broken zip and a shadow where some meatza I was eating fell on the sleeve. Another part of me feels guilty about starting a bonfire late at night in my elderly neighbour's garden. It's so hard to know the right thing to do, when life doesn't come with a guidebook.

My sister Rosie is naturally very pretty, and she is also very good at putting on make-up. It seems unfair, doesn't it? What if I tell you she is kind, funny and clever as well? If you're anything like me, you'll stamp your feet and become incandescent with rage at the realisation that one person can have all of these qualities. I worked on my personality for many years, in the mistaken belief that being witty and nice would serve me in my quest to beat the beauties around me. Then I found out that most of them were naturally witty and nice, and didn't spend their time in their room listening to Radiohead and imagining some ultimate battle where only one woman could emerge victorious.

But back to Rosie – she did have some make-up training when she went to beauty therapy school. She used my mother as a model for her exams. That was interesting, because my mother doesn't usually wear make-up and Rosie had to demonstrate every technique she had learned on her face, all at once. She made my mother look like a geisha. A middle-aged geisha, off-duty and in tracksuit bottoms. We couldn't stop staring at her as she poured our tea and sat back demurely on her heels. Rosie cannot bear to watch me put on make-up. She says that I rummage around the bag, pull out whatever is inside and smear it on carelessly, like I'm finger-painting in play school. She's kind of right.

You see, I think it's dishonest to use make-up to just look like a better version of yourself. I believe its purpose should primarily be decorative. Don't try to camouflage your skin, unless you want to blend in with a pre-teen's bedroom, all glittery and pink. A lot of brides – sorry – Brides want 'the natural look', so that their groom can tell which one they are. I think they are wasting an opportunity. They will have a make-up artist on hand and 100 per cent guaranteed attention from everyone at the wedding. They should take advantage of that, and get their make-up done in a beautifully unique way.

If I ever achieve my dream of being a Bride – one of Earth's angels – I will get a stunning job done on my face. I will shade all around my eyes to make them look absolutely gigantic. I will use brown eye shadow to play up their dull blueness. They will be azure, all-seeing globes, swivelling around the cathedral of my head and taking it all in. I'll ask the make-up artist if she has any ideas on how to make my cheeks sharp like razor clams. And a Bride's mouth must say: *I have chosen and been chosen.* A big circle of lipstick should be applied to emphasise the 'oh' sound therein. Finally, I will stick a few diamanté teardrops to my face – because a crying Bride is an unforgettable Bride.

The train from Cobh to Cork takes twenty-four minutes, and that is exactly how long it takes my sister Daisy to do her make-up. By Little Island, her foundation and concealer are in place. She's applying mascara with an impressively steady hand as we shudder past Fota Island, and blotting her fuchsia lips as the train pulls into Kent station. Daisy works in a market, and I think it's great that people get to see a vivid and bright face when they're being handed their bread. Kurt Vonnegut appreciated the lady in his local post office making an effort with her hair and make-up – he never knew what she'd look like on any given day, and that pleased him. I'm sure lots of other great people are the same with Daisy. I, for one, love her jewel-coloured face, so cheerful and pretty.

Here is my hotly anticipated guide to who's who in the world of cosmetics:

Mascara

Make-up is supposed to mimic the effects of being turned on. I'm not so sure. My neck flushes and my cheeks burn more in business meetings than in the bedroom. Aren't I so tame, thinking I can only be turned on in the bedroom? I need to open my mind and consider the infinite sexiness of the hot press or that triangle under the stairs where we keep the mop. Anyway, when I'm turned on, the spider veins on my cheekbones don't coat themselves in taupe-coloured shimmer – I wish! That said, mascara does make it seem like each of your eyelashes has an erection.

Eyeliner

My friend's sister uses a credit card to get the black line just right. I freestyle and it works out, though sometimes if I'm on some form of lurching public transport, I don't manage to get the thickness completely the same on both eyes. That gives the impression that I have one eye bigger than the other, lending me a peculiar look I like to call 'the dead doll who can walk around'. Eyeliner is worth that risk, it really plays up your eyes. Beauty experts always tell us to play up one feature, and one feature only: usually your eyes or your mouth. They never say what to do if neither of these happens to be your strong point.

Not that I have anything to worry about – my eyes are endlessly fascinating. You know how some people have eyes as blue as cornflowers in the sun? I pity those people for their conventional, easily imagined colouring. My eyes are far more interesting. They are the colour of a gun, if that gun was made from a sort of blue metal. They are the colour of the Irish Sea just after a minor oil spill. They have the trails of a few Spanish trawlers running through them and locked within is a glimpse of the infinite sadness of all Irish people crossing that sea, away from the old country. My eyes are naturally sad-looking. When I'm happy or sad or not thinking about whether I'm happy or sad, my eyes remain sad-looking. That's why – and you can do this too if you have downcast peepers – I use eyeliner to make them turn up into a smile. An inauthentic-looking, throwback smile from the 1950s, but a smile nonetheless. Glance at me and you'll think: *There goes a happy washerwoman, whistling away with a smile in her eyes*. Look closer and you'll say: *There goes a reasonably content woman with expertly applied eyeliner and a fantastic butt*. I'll thank you not to break me down into parts like that – but I'll also thank you for the compliments.

Bronzer

How can you achieve that relaxed, sun-warmed glow without exposing yourself to harmful rays of the actual brutish sun? The answer is, you can't. How can you make it look like I've dipped a boar-bristle brush into some brown glitter and then swiped it across your T-zone? The answer is that you can do exactly that, and it will be apparent to all. Actual bronzing of faces rarely occurs in the natural landscape that is an Irish woman's skin. It's like when a pretentious architect builds a spaceship-type house on the Burren – it's the future showing up the past, and nobody wins.

Powder

I have loved powder for a long time. It's one of the reasons I think there was a mix-up and I'm alive in the wrong era. I should be around in sixteenth-century Paris. Instead of bathing, I would simply use powder to disguise my filth. I would never catch a cold and I would sit in bed and eat Turkish delight directly from my maid's hands. Neither of us would feel weird about it, because that was the way back then. Not like nowadays, where you get a cup in a fast-food restaurant and you have to bloody fill it up yourself. Body powder and face powder is the same, except face powder has some skin-coloured dye in it. Its purpose is to 'set' your face, so you have to be careful what expression you're making as you apply it. I shoot for sanguine, stay away from horrified and usually end up somewhere along the lines of worried but fundamentally placid. That particular look? Drives men wild.

Blush

I am getting on in years, so tend to use a *lot* of blush. That, combined with a little romper suit with big buttons and my hair all done in ringlets, makes me look like a little girl again. My sister Rosie has a complicated relationship with blush. Since she was a tiny baby, she's had unbearably cute, bright-pink cheeks. Strangers would often smile when they saw her and say *Hello, Rosy* – making her think the world was a magical place, where everybody knew her name. Then she grew to resent it. We told her she was lucky her name wasn't Gonzo or Knockers but she still turned against her pink cheeks, because they gave her name away and also because they made her look 'too rural'. In her teens, she began painting over them with a special green paste to tone down the pink, letting that dry in and then applying a layer of brown foundation. She continues doing so to this day, always finishing off her cheeks with a dusting of powdery-pink blush to make them Rosie again, but urban.

Lip liner

Allow me to share this short verse with you: *To L.L. My sweetheart. My friend. My keeper of secrets, my darling boy. You know how I feel about my sharp little mouth, my lips the size and shape of a €2 coin edge. You help me.*

And it does. Lipliner slinks up to me and giggles, then gets serious as it asks, concern in its pointy eyes: *Why should you put up with those lips you've been given? When I am here for you and can help you get the lips you feel you deserve?* I can only answer by grabbing lip liner by the neck, sharpening it and happily drawing a generous circle of it all around my old mouth to create a giant new one that better represents my personality. If films about aliens have taught me anything, it's that we are all evolving into creatures with tiny zip-up mouths and big shark eyes. I'm halfway there, which makes me feel conflicted. It means I don't have a sultry pout, but it also hints at the fact that I am probably ahead of the posse in other ways too – like being emotionally in tune. Just today I saw a woman crying at a bus stop, and told an old man standing nearby that he should go and ask her if she was alright.

Lipstick

Ever since I was eight years old, my definition of being an adult has been someone that a) has a boyfriend, and b) wears lipstick. I'd like to say right now: *Congratulations, Maeve, you passed the test. You have had boyfriends and worn lipstick. You won the challenges. You are a grown-up.* You know me though – always striving to be better. I've added more qualities now that I have yet to achieve. When I do, I will finally become what doctors call 'an actual grown-up'. Such qualities include:

- Being able to drive a car or a truck.

- Cleaning the kitchen, then sighing to myself and saying: *Now, doesn't the whole place feel much better?*

- Managing to hold it together when a bird gets in the house.

- Becoming a parent or a grandparent.

Despite my expertise, I have mixed feelings when it comes to trying and buying make-up myself. As you have probably guessed, I am extremely fond of make-up artists and salespeople because they *really* brighten the place up. The rules of department stores generally state that employees have to wear a uniform of all-black clothes, two sizes too small for them. Make-up salespeople react against this austerity by hanging things off, sticking things to and generally colouring in, the front of their heads. They are like those dark monkeys with bright paradise faces. They're like beautiful robot dolls with heightened features and hyper-real hairstyles. I feel giddy when I'm in their presence, like anything is possible when it comes to my face.

The excitement sours though and I get angry with myself when I catch sight of my own boring reflection. I curse my lack of imagination and try to make up for it by buying inappropriate items. I want to impress these big, gaudy birds and live up to their sherbety ideal. Once I bought a yellow eyeshadow for €17. Another time I almost bought a glittering black lipstick – but one of the pretty-monkey-gaudy-birds felt sorry for me and stopped me. At some make-up counters, you have to book weeks in advance if you want to get your make-up done there, even on a Wednesday. The last time I tried to get an appointment at a popular city-centre counter, a thin boy wearing peacock-feather eyelashes said, not unkindly: *I don't even have to look in the book to tell you that's not gonna happen.*

I sometimes dream of a parallel life as a make-up girl, where I'd make spots and wrinkles and ruddiness vanish and replace them with red, pillowy smiles and glowing, shimmering eyes. I'd spend all day using my mad skills with a set of brushes, making grateful people look like cartoon versions of themselves, in a good way. And every night, right after I'd meticulously removed my own make-up, I'd go to sleep happy, clutching my lip liner, my love.

I can totally see why
my parents loved me

Something about standing alone in a hairnet and a paper thong, waiting for my spray tan to dry made me realise the truth about the first boy that ever asked me out.

My regular beauty therapist is a tiny, kind lady, who chats away and makes eye contact even when she's doing unspeakably personal things to me – which somehow makes those bizarro rituals seem perfectly normal. She was, thoughtlessly, away on honeymoon when this incident occurred. I was in trouble with the new beautician as soon as I arrived, because my back was sweating and she'd had to reapply the tan there twice. I told her not to bother, that I wasn't planning on wearing any backless gowns that night – but she tut-tutted and said I shouldn't have run on my way there. I said I had had to or I would have been late, but she said that it would have been better to have been a few minutes late than to arrive sweating, because now the tan mightn't take.

Generally, I think sweating is great. It means you're doing something – not thinking about something, or thinking about doing something. In my boxing class my partner once apologised to me for sweating. I reminded her that that's what we were there for, and hit her with an especially hard uppercut.

I couldn't punch the beautician, though. I just apologised for almost a full minute over the hiss of the tan gun. Although I couldn't help feeling that, as someone who frequently waxes men's balls, she seemed unduly upset by such a harmless bodily function. Eventually her professionalism kicked in, and she said it was fine, but that I'd have to wait a bit longer for it to dry. I made a note to not go back to that salon again, and it was as if she read my mind; she left me standing in my vertical plastic beauty coffin without a magazine. As punishment.

That's when I remembered what had happened with John Fitzpatrick. He was the dreamiest bad boy in first year. Everything he did was cool, including having crutches. It takes a certain sort of hero to make something so intrinsically weak into something everybody wants – like the first time Tupac tied his bandana into those little bunny ears, and nobody laughed. In 1992, crutches became the biggest status symbol there was among thirteen-year-olds on the island of Cobh. John smelled of smoke and reigned supreme, and the boys wanted to be him, while the girls weren't exactly sure what they wanted to do to him. It involved getting rescued by him, then somehow achieving a state of euphoria, with the other girls being jealous but respectful.

For the first few weeks of secondary school, everyone jostled for position and I couldn't figure out where I should land. Everything was huge and different compared to my primary school, where I'd never been in a classroom without at least two of my siblings. I wasn't making friends as easily as I thought I would, maybe because I was almost completely devoid of any shred of self-awareness. My parents had successfully tricked me into thinking I was, in my mother's words, an *exotic butterfly*. My father talked a lot about how pretty I was, and how I'd break hearts when I grew up. Looking at photos of myself from that time, I see a smiley chubster with a crew cut and headgear, who spent her free time writing overly personal letters to political prisoners in East Timor. I can totally see why my parents loved me, but I was far from an exotic butterfly.

One breaktime, early on in the year, John's best friend Philip approached my table. He was a classic wingman – small, devoted and funny, usually in a mean way. He said John had asked him to ask me if I'd get off with him: John wanted to kiss me. I reacted with a scandalised: *Ah … no way! I don't even know him!* But my heart was pounding. I looked for the girls I'd been eating lunch with, but they had vanished. Didn't bother me, this new joint was playing right into my hands! Everything was falling into place, just as my parents said it would. A month into first year and the most popular boy in school had asked me to get off with him! It was like clockwork.

I watched, as Philip went back to the huddle around John and told him the bad news. This was followed quickly by a roar of laughter, and I shook my head. They were cruel friends to John, laughing at his rejection. He'd have the last laugh, I decided there and then – because I would kiss him!

I would wait until we were officially going out, and I would totally kiss him. That particular day preceded an incredible two-month period, during which John sent not only Philip, but a number of the boys in first year my way, with various requests. *John wants to know where you get your hair cut ... John said, will you meet him downtown after school? ... John said he can't believe you keep saying no, and will you please meet him?* They meant *meet* meet. He sure was persistent. I batted away the requests. I think the official term is 'playing hard to get', but really, I wanted to arrange things with John himself. He was always surrounded by people, and never made eye contact with me. I added 'actually really shy' to my list of his attributes, and made a plan. My big idea was to get to talk to him alone, see if he wanted to call out to my house and listen to Bob Marley's *Legend*, and maybe help wash my father's car ...

The beautician zipped in for a second, pressed her fingertips to my shoulder, said *Still tacky*, and left. I could hear her talking to her colleague outside and I tried to make out what they were saying, but I couldn't. Beauticians talk in low, reassuring tones – like volunteers in a hospice.

I was just in one class with John – Geography. He was often sent outside the door for bad behaviour. It's a funny theory teachers have – that if someone is annoying, you should put them out of the room. The student happily misses out on their education and comes back brazen as ever, but you've not had to look at them for ten minutes, and I guess that can make all the difference.

One sleepy Tuesday afternoon, Mr O'Shea caught John drawing vaginas on Philip's notes, and immediately sent him to the corridor for ten minutes. I desperately wanted to go outside and speak to him, for us to be alone for the first time, to discuss our compatibility and for me to ask if he was around on Saturday. I tried everything I could think of to misbehave. I didn't put my hand up when the teacher asked what types of rock there are, even though I could have. Igneous, sedimentary and metamorphic – my brother had taught me a handy trick for memorising them – *I Smell Mars bars!* Take a moment if you will, to absorb this postscript – Oliver grew up to be a geologist, and to this day, I really can smell Mars bars, from up to four feet away.

I passed a note to my friend Claire – hoping to get caught in the act. The teacher didn't see. The page was blank anyway, and Claire looked at me quizzically. Though she was looking at everyone quizzically in those days, as she had yet to get the hang of plucking her eyebrows. I was out of ideas on how to be bad. These days, of course, I can think of loads of ways to get kicked out of class. I could have lit up a cigar or drawn vaginas on my notes, or answered questions in the style of Louis Armstrong: *Say cat, you want to know what Satchmo says? It's glacial!* I always think of these things too late.

In the end, I asked if I could go to the toilet. Mr O'Shea gave me a pass: an oblong piece of wood made by some of the dozier children in woodwork class. I hated holding toilet passes, and gripped this one with my sleeve, thinking about all of the germs on that bit of wood, living their lives

174

and loving the filthy hands of adolescents. It was worth it, though, to spent some alone time with the hottest brat in Cobh.

John was leaning against the radiator, looking annoyed and totally handsome, his crutches on the ground. He didn't notice me. I leaned on the radiator beside him and sighed. My sigh meant: *Oh man, I hate this planet and its bullshit fakers, sometimes I think I'm the only one who gets it – but I know you do too. You and me, we get it. Now, you may ask me out.* John just studied the carpet tiles, and time stretched out. Eventually I said: *Mr O' Shea is such a pain*, and John finally looked at me and asked: *You get kicked out?* I said, rolling my eyes: *Yeah, kind of.* Then he saw the pass, and smiled in a way I didn't understand until sixteen years later, as I stood, still tacky, in a tanning booth in Dublin.

Just like that, I was floored. One humiliation often recalls another, but why the hell did it take me all these years to realise that John Fitzpatrick was actually being a classic bully? Throughout my entire teens, he was the only person to ask me out. I sometimes wondered about that, but hadn't clicked until that moment that it was all a big joke. I wondered if the gap between how I perceived myself and how others perceived me was still that wide. Was there some link between that gap and the crazy ritual I was putting myself through that very day?

What the hell was I doing, anyway, paying a stranger dressed like a nurse to colour me in with a gun? I felt sorry for myself and also furious. I'd imagine that is a very common combination of feelings in beauty parlours around the world.

Hot tears pricked my eyes but I didn't cry, because that would have left two tracks of paleness down my face and gotten me into more trouble with that damn beautician – if she ever came back.

Sales ladies can be chillingly perceptive

A friend of mine, Katie, is very beautiful and I've noticed that I try very hard to please her. Something about a symmetrical face and pretty hair brings out the creep in me. It doesn't matter if the glorious one is male or female, young or old – I find myself lurking in their vicinity, watching them closely, trying to anticipate their needs. *Water?* I'll ask anxiously. *Tiramisu? Trip to the pictures?* With a sweep of their perfect eyelashes, I'll know if I've got it right or not. My prize is to bask a while longer in the glow of their flawless skin.

I'm better at hiding it these days: at thirteen, I would scare people away. Once, on a bus, I offered to read aloud to an eighteen-year-old Roman God from my brother's school. He seemed under the weather – his square shoulders hunched in, his aquiline nose a little red. He was horrified at my whispered suggestion and moved seats immediately.

More often than not, Katie wants to go shopping. It's her favourite thing to do, so we go to clothes shops and walk around them in circles, waiting for something to 'grab' her. She has piles of clothes that have successfully grabbed her at one point, and now lie in a drawer, shivering in hope as they await their next outing. I don't enjoy shopping myself: I think it's boring and the air in shopping centres makes me feel both sleepy and anxious. I currently own two pairs of jeans and one pair of jeggings, which are like jeans but thirty per cent more unflattering. I own two dresses and six jumpers. Six seems like a lot, but three of them are stripy, two of them are identical and grey, and one of them has a large rip in the back from when I crawled under a fence. I should buy more clothes, to make my wardrobe less like an eight-year-old boy's – but, like I said, I find shopping dispiriting.

With Katie, though, it's different. Dresses slip on and come to life as she spins around the changing room, we laugh and I tell her she *must* get them. Her little feet kick off her shoes and she mock-plods in fur-lined boots. I can't take my eyes off her, and tell her breathlessly that she looks like a Russian princess. She looks at me funny. I act casual then, tell her the colour is not great. Remind myself that we are two friends: equal, for all she knows. It's not like my face has been bitten off by an ape or anything (touch wood), but I can't help myself from fawning over beautiful people. My sycophantic tendencies are obvious to others too. Sales ladies can be chillingly perceptive. One time, as I helped Katie carry the evening dress she was buying to the till, the lady said brightly: *So that'll be €230 when you're ready – who's taking care of that?* As if I was a sugar daddy getting his doll a treat for keeping herself nice.

I find it hard to believe that really beautiful people experience pain, rejection and shame like everybody else. I imagine their lives to be long, sunny days by the sea, not worrying about hairy legs or back fat. They can just relax, with their glowing eyes and even skin tone, soaking up the rays that won't give them pink stripes on their arms. In my head, they sail through red lights and nobody admonishes them. Queues for cash machines part respectfully, to allow them to go first. The chef peeps out from the kitchen to have a look, then plates up the finest turbot in their honour. They don't notice any of this, because it's normal to them.

I'm wrong, of course. I've been studying Katie for a long time now, and see that she misses trains, walks into dog poo, gets dumped and has period cramps just as often as I do. Handsome old men fall over and break their hips just as often as plain old men do. I just can't help feeling that the doctors are nicer to the handsome ones. I would be, if I was their doctor. I wouldn't treat the other ones roughly or anything – I just wouldn't go that extra mile for them. The extra mile being a smile and an explanation of the surgical procedure required. Similarly, I know if I was a teacher*, I would favour the pretty children in my classroom. I would let the cuter kids off homework if they got a particularly great haircut, and I would side with them in schoolyard arguments with the uglier ones.

My friend Fiona is a teacher (in the conventional sense), and she told me that there are twin girls in her class. Are they identical? No, they are not. In fact, nothing could be further from the truth. One of them is petite and luminous; the other is hulking and dour. I want to meet them and follow them

---

* I hope that you already think of me as a teacher, of sorts. A spirit guide, a shaman, if you will, leading you people towards the Land of Chuckles. (I also hope you don't mind me referring to you as 'you people'.)

around, to witness how different their experiences are. Fiona won't allow me to, so I quiz her instead. Does the frumpy one have any talents or abilities her gorgeous sister doesn't? No, in fact the great beauty plays basketball and sings in the choir, while the poor lummox doesn't even do drama. Do they get along? The beautiful angel is very kind to the ugly devil, who does not reciprocate but seethes quietly instead.

I asked Fiona which one she prefers, and she said she likes the beautiful one the most. She was at pains to point out that it wasn't because she is more beautiful. It was because she is smiley and sweet-natured – unlike her sister, who is constantly simmering with a barely contained rage that nobody can explain.

Meanwhile,
in a deli uptown

My friend Miranda is a big-time lawyer. My other friend is a sexy older woman called Samantha. Charlotte, an uptight brunette, completes our gang. Together, we pick listlessly at food and reinforce gender stereotypes. Hollywood, are you listening?

Before you commission a trilogy of films and design a line of character dildos, I must confess that only Miranda is real. She was the first friend I made when I moved from my co-educational secondary school to a convent school when I was 14. Miranda studied extra hard in college, got a first, aced her solicitor's exams and has worked really hard for ten years. She works so much that she only has time for two hobbies. One is squash and the other is downplaying her career achievements.

Miranda and I have lunch together every fortnight or so. In a deli uptown, I ask her how things are going.

Good – for now at least … It's going good – well, OK; it's going OK. Kind of busy at the moment.

Didn't you have an interview for partner?

Oh yeah, yeah actually I did, a few weeks ago. She looks pained. *Grand – like I got it, so it went good.*

Even a clown like me realises partner is a big deal. It was basically all Michael Douglas wanted in *War of the Roses*. So I cheer: *We should be celebrating! We should get ice cream, or get our eyebrows tinted, or something, no?*

No! My God. It's not a big thing. They just felt sorry for me and there was nobody else around, really.

The firm she works for is one of the biggest in Ireland; I checked during one of those afternoons when you sit down and idly Google your friends. *Miranda, why would they feel sorry for you? They obviously think you're brilliant, if they made you partner and you're only thirty.*

She grimaces as if she is about to be sick. *Oh I don't know. Look, how're you anyway? How's the book going?*

I am flooded with self-doubt at the question, and feel my brow tighten up. *Good, it's going grand … I don't know … It's not going great. I just hope it'll be OK.*

She looks at me with her sympathetic, clever eyes. *Of course it will. It'll be great – you're a good writer.*

And you're a good solicitor, you must be. Your firm is one of the biggest in the country, and was recently awarded the Ireland Client Service Award of the year by Cusacks Europe.

She says she doesn't remember telling me that. To distract her, I quickly show her a photo of my nephew wearing bunny ears. I know what our problem is. We're both afraid we'll get found out – that the sands will shift under us, and the world will see that we are not good enough. It's so lame, feeling like that. I look at the table next to us where two suited men are eating steak, and I think darkly: *They're probably congratulating themselves on how great they are, because they don't have a constant, underlying sense of panic about their place in the world – because they are not women.*

This is possibly very unfair. Maybe the portly duo's conversation is also based around hiding their ambition. Maybe they too are putting themselves down – maybe they are even calling themselves fat, to boot. Me no know; me no hear them!

I just wish there was a drug myself and Miranda could take, to put pep in our step, some bounce in our flounce, a little proud self-belief in our hearts. I know what you're thinking: *Wake up, Maeve – cocaine does exactly that!* But cocaine is hardly a practical, long-term solution for someone like me, who gets heart palpitations after a cup of coffee.

I'll have to come up with something, though. Hopefully, as we get older, Miranda and I will simply become more sure of ourselves. I don't think there is ever any danger of us getting 'up ourselves'. Being up yourself is bad news, here in Ireland. It means liking yourself and not being shy about saying so. People who are up themselves are regarded with deep suspicion by those in the wider community, who whisper things like: *If he was a bar of chocolate, he'd eat himself.* And so he should. What kind of maniac is a bar of chocolate and *doesn't* eat himself? What should he do instead – wait to be eaten by somebody else? Melt? Sit at a meeting and have his neck go all red and his voice get super-high when it's his turn to say something?

For now, I remind Miranda of the one veiled reference to feminism on display at our conservative all-girls secondary school. On the wall outside the principal's office hung a small poster, which said: *Remember, Ginger Rogers did everything Fred Astaire did, only backwards and in heels*. It made our heads spin – I'll tell you that for nothing – when we thought about all of the things we could do, only backwards *and in heels*.

A bulldog with ham arms

Last night I tried on a vest top belonging to my sister Raedi. I suppose I was poking around her room. She was out with friends, leaving me home alone, so it serves her right. The vest top was slightly too small for me. I didn't toss it aside and set about continuing the fashion show that I had been planning. Instead, I sat crossly on her bed and I thought: *Well of course it doesn't fit – why would it fit a bulldog with ham arms?*

This bulldog with ham arms I was referring to? That was me. Maeve Higgins – a regular human girl with arms made out of muscle and bone and fat and sinew and water and blood, covered by skin with some freckles on it. Just a normal pair of arms attached to a non-canine pair of shoulders. My arms are really nothing like ham and my body is really nothing like a bulldog's. Some days, I just think things like that.

I'm not the only one. My friend Edel told me she calls herself a cunt sometimes. I tell her that's awful, that she's not a cunt, and she certainly wouldn't speak to anybody else like that, even if they were a cunt. She agrees that it is quite a full-on thing to say, but adds: *In fairness, I say it in an encouraging way, like if I'm in the gym and I don't think I can finish out a set, then I kind of scream at myself 'Come on, you stupid cunt – you can do better than this!'*

This trash-talking is not exclusive to Edel and me. It is widespread, so much so that I am writing a play about it. I am not a big fan of going to the theatre. I can't help thinking that all of the people on stage are just acting. That said, I am working on this one incredibly moving and powerful play. It is not finished, but I will share it with you now in its rawest state. Art is exciting when it's by the seat of its pants, no? Yes. So, hold your breath and be part of the magic …

Scene One

INTERIOR: *A cave with some nice cave paintings on the wall and a cavewoman sitting cross-legged on the floor, crying as she clicks two pieces of flint together. A caveman walks in and frowns at her.*

CAVEMAN: What wrong?

CAVEWOMAN: Me big leg. Me sad.

CAVEMAN: You good fire. You good mother. You sweet lovin'.

CAVEWOMAN: No matter. Me fat idiot.

Later in the play…

EXTERIOR: *Dickensian London street. An elegant debutante is scurrying along and catches sight of her reflection in the window of an inn. Her little face, which had been alight with anticipation, darkens.*

Soliloquy begins:

Well, well, young Mistress Dimbleby – off to the ball? I'm in the finest silks, sent from the Orient by my dear old Amah and fashioned into a pretty gown by Mrs Hurst's quick hands, and yet I look a damn fool. My hair – so limp. No curls like Mamma and Beth – and my skin is brown, like a simple farm boy. I am a swarthy, flat-haired rake of a girl and I have no business coming out in society – I am ashamed of myself.

Scene ends.

Aren't you stirred up by the emotional punchiness? I am. Get ready for a stunning musical close. The finale happens on a pirate ship on the Indian Ocean and will be sung loudly by a pretty female pirate as she ransacks the ship with her colleagues.

FEMALE PIRATE: Forget about the treasure chest, I'd be 'appy wiv a normal chest. I ain't got no bosoms, none at all, it's no bloody wonder I'm a rubbish pirate. Yo-ho-ho on the high seas? More like a flat calm, matey.

And … scene.

Crowd.Goes.Wild.

On the way to pick up my inevitable award, with my hair all done, I check my teeth for lipstick, and the mean old voice starts at me again: *Uh-oh, chin alert. How many chins does one chubster need? Eleven?* And so on. Thoughts like this leave me feeling totally deflated. They create an alternative Jedward – terrible twins of pain and self-doubt – and they

187

do nobody any good. They don't spur you on to improve or find a way towards being content: they just shove you further down into your wringing despondency. You're no use to anyone like that. Women who hate themselves are no fun at all. I like inflated ones. I trust you know what I mean – not inflated like sex dolls or egomaniacs. I mean, I like to be around confident women, who live outside the little prison of self-absorbed self-loathing. They're the greatest, and I'm trying hard to become one of them.

As a genius comedian, I used to do a lot of jokes about my weight. None of them were great, except for this one: *I'd like to lose weight. Not too much, just enough to get back to my original weight. When I was born, I was eight-and-a-half pounds.*

OK, it's not great, but it is kind of funny. I put it to bed, though, with all the other fat jokes. I had to question the wisdom of pulling myself to pieces on stage night after night, despite or maybe because of the fact that doing so always got laughs. I also realised that not every comedian relies on putting themselves down to get laughs. There are lots of different styles of comedy available for us to choose from. Examples include racist impressions, classic vaudeville and general, angry ranting. I plan on exploring all of these in my next one-woman show, working title: *Me So High on da Sweet Herb that … Whoopsie, Didn't See that Banana Skin! I Bet the Fucking Government Put it There, Bunch of Crooks!*

It's going to be a hit, I'm telling you – it's my ticket on the gravy train, self-esteem intact, all the way to the top.

Snug and shapely

When we were children, my mother used to play her Bonnie Tyler record really loud, and we would all dance around the bedroom. The downstairs bedroom, that is – the one my aunt had mysteriously painted purple in the early 1970s and, even more mysteriously, my parents didn't repaint until the late 1980s. My favourite song was 'Holding Out for a Hero'. I still use it as a reference point for new boyfriends. *Are you strong?* I ask them. *Are you fast? Are you fresh from the fight?* If they hesitate for even a second, I'm on to the next one.

Lately, my heroes have been arriving in unexpected ways – mainly in the form of 37-year-old women. They've got it going on. I like them a lot. I think they're cool and I want to be like them. I'm crushing on them and I don't care who knows it. I have been increasingly impressed with every single 37-year-old woman I've met, ever since I started keeping track of my favourite groups of people over two years ago.

Traditionally I have responded well to chubby babies, dorky pre-teens with spiky opinions, and witty gay men. I also gravitate towards easy-going smokers and funny Australians. And, predictably, I still hanker after the streetwise Hercules type mentioned by Bonnie Tyler. I have space for all of them in my life, but right now it is the 37-year-old woman who comes out swinging, ready and able to punch her way straight to my heart. Here is why:

1. These women know a thing or two about a thing or two. They have lived, and it's not so much that they know a few cities or languages or have done loads of different jobs or have been in jail that makes them interesting – it's because they know themselves. Not totally – not enough to be jaded – but just enough to be calm and steady. I try not to blow whichever way the wind blows, but it's hard. I hear myself agreeing when someone insists that Ben & Jerry's Coconutterly Fair is their best flavour, and that we should get it, even though I way prefer Core Dough-Ble Whammy. Even on the crucial topic of ice cream, I don't always state how I feel.

Case Study: Eavan, 37

Eavan knows what she thinks, and I defy any of you to stop her from telling the world. Here are some of the things I've heard her say that have made me jump a bit and also want to be more like her:

–   On a mutual friend appearing on a TV reality dating show: *I don't find that interesting. What else can we talk about?* A revelation: we are allowed to put a quick stop to a boring conversation and not go through the motions like monkeys with miniature cymbals.

- On a man not pulling his weight in her office: *It's a pain, but the situation will be resolved quickly because I'm his boss.* Yikes! I believe you, because you are like a combination of Cagney, Lacey *and* Lieutenant Samuels.

- On an underperforming waitress: *She can tip her toes.* Pow! She does it again! I tip everyone, even the rude ones, in the hope that they'll feel guilty for not being nicer to me. That madness is over now – thanks to Eavan.

2. The way I see it, 37-year-old women are usually headed in a direction they have chosen, and dressed for success. And I don't mean a pantsuit and glasses – though that would be fine. I mean that these women are usually doing something they care about, and not faffing around, thinking about it. Or faffing around, regretting not doing it. And they are also wearing clothes that suit them.

Case study: Sara, 37

Sara's jeans are just perfect. They are not super-tight – the kind that make your legs look like a mixture of sausages and rashers. They are not too loose – the kind that make you look like you've taken a break from feeding the pigs to read the *Sun*. They are just right: snug and shapely.*

---

* Please don't steal my two favourite children's names before I get a chance to use them. I can't wait to meet you, Snug! And you too, Shapely. You are the best twin boys a mother could dream of!

Sara also wears a parka jacket with a furry hood, as popularised by the 1990s girl group All Saints. The parka jacket looks incredible on her: serious, relaxed and fun, all at the same time. And that is what she is!

I don't know where Sara gets her clothes and I don't want to find out, because they are part of her mystique. Mystique was another girl band from the 1990s. An important girl group *not* represented in the outfit choices of my 37-year-old women friends is B*Witched, whose distinctive double-denim look has yet to be adopted by any of them.

3. They can spot sexism a mile away. Maybe because they were born in the slightly liberated 1970s, or maybe because they have educated themselves on this sneaky, rotten phenomenon – either way, it's always a relief when a 37-year-old woman untangles a situation by calling it like it is. Sexism: it's not sexy, but 37-year-old women totally are.

Case study: Emer, 37

A few years ago a comedian told me he'd love to book me as his support on a big tour he was doing. Then he said he couldn't, because if he did, then he and I would end up spending a lot of time together, and people would assume there was something going on between us. He said he hoped I understood – but I didn't. I felt confused, and like it was somehow my fault that my career wasn't moving on up. Then I talked to my 37-year-old friend Emer and she said: *That's pure sexist!* She is from Cork, too. What a woman.

4. They give advice in a deft and effective way. The way I take in advice depends totally on how it's delivered. When someone sort of barks instructions crossly, I feel a bit hopeless. I listen and arrange my face in a way that says: *I will make a concerted effort to do exactly as you say* – but I don't, because I lose confidence in my ability to do anything. Most 37-year-old women have read a range of self-help literature and have worked on their own flaws tirelessly, and without the self-loathing present in their younger sisters. This makes them considered and kind. Their suggestions often lead to manageable, humane solutions. I'll drink to that! (Drinking has never been presented to me by a 37-year-old woman as a manageable, humane solution.)

Case Study: Una, 37

I was having man trouble. By that, I mean I was seeing a man who was far too busy to have a girlfriend. Boy, oh boy, was he busy. Too busy to return my calls until, like, 3 a.m. on a Friday morning! I read once that Barack Obama gets up early, does some exercise, has breakfast, goes to the office, does his work, then heads home and watches TV with his wife and kids. It seemed strange that this other man, not the President of the United States, absolutely did not have one minute to spare, especially considering he was unemployed at the time. I never asked him about his time management issues. I couldn't, because I wasn't his official girlfriend. Also, I was *so* busy myself, dreaming up ways of hoodwinking his heart and convincing him that I'd be no trouble at all, if he would just fall in love with me.

In the middle of this endless non-relationship, I had lunch with my friend Una. She asked me how it was going and I told her it was great. I said we had been out at the weekend and we were getting on great, but we were both up the walls and I wasn't sure I wanted something serious anyway. Then I studied the menu. With a line of questioning that included times and locations, she gently removed my head from the sand and set about restoring my self-esteem. I stopped seeing Mr Can't-Talk-Le-Roux. The very next week I met my husband on a yacht. The last bit isn't true. I actually met him at the perfume counter at Arnotts.

That's not true either – I don't have a husband. *I'm too busy playin' like the playa I is. You can't stop me playin' – no way, no how. Playin' in my blood, boo. Ain't nothing you can do.* When I talked to Una about using rap as a way to talk myself up and not be taken for a fool again, she told me that writing and reciting my own was probably unnecessary, but that listening to self-aggrandising MCs would work wonders. She was right again. I don't know the science behind it, but there is nothing like a blast of Biggie Smalls, rhyming over some beats about how great he is, to instil a little confidence in a girl.

As you examine my reasons for singling out this little group in the population, you may find yourself saying: *Hold up, Maeverino – I'm a 37-year-old man and I qualify under the whole 'good parent/knows stuff' section.* Or maybe you are reading this and thinking: *Woah there, Maeverly – I'm ninety-six and I absolutely dress for success; I also know sexism, because I was a suffragette.*

Look, I'm sure you all have *some* of the qualities I've mentioned, but you don't have them *all*. The only people who have them all, for one magical year, are 37-year-old women. And to think, all going to plan, I am going to actually be one of them myself! I'm tempted to ask someone to bop me on the head and wake me up on my thirty-seventh birthday – but then I'd miss a whole seven years' worth of hanging out with 37-year-old women, as well as the other experiences that will form me into one. So I guess the best thing is to keep going the way I'm going and stay in awe of my special ladies, until one day I myself become THE ULTIMATE DREAMGIRL37™.

A couple of times I've pretended to have a boyfriend

As a seventeen-year-old au pair in New York, I looked after four children all week, like a mother would, if she didn't have an au pair. The children's actual mother would sometimes feel guilty about this, and bring me shopping to an outlet mall. It was nice to get a break from the kids, but I don't like shopping. I find shopping malls in Ireland too big and airless for comfort, let alone American shopping malls, let alone American *Outlet* shopping malls.

Dundrum Town Centre, the biggest shopping mall in Ireland, is a mewling kitten compared to the roaring panther that is the Woodbury Common Outlet Mall. There are a dozen car parks stretched across acres of land. Each store takes up a football pitch. Thousands of dresses hang mutely, waiting to be chosen by glassy-eyed consumers as they amble around the aisles, punch-drunk from all the goods. They fuel themselves with coffee and something sugary every two hours, then continue to stroll around numbly. Soft, easy-listening music is piped all around, inside and out, right out to the perimeters. This might sound relaxing, and it is – kind of. But think about this: easy-listening music is played to cows in abattoirs too, so they won't tense up right before they get killed. See what I'm saying? Wake up, zombies! Last season's Ralph Lauren shirts are going to make you into burgers!

Anyway, it was in an underwear shop the size of Croke Park that I pretended to have a boyfriend for the first time. I was buying knickers and a bra, and the woman at the till said: *You know these aren't a pair, right? They don't match – is that OK?*

And I said: *Oh – he won't notice.* I really emphasised the 'he' and gave the saleswoman what I hoped was a knowing look between grown-up women. She grimaced a bit and didn't say another word to me: the hulking Irish virgin standing before her, suddenly embarrassed.

Most recently – Wednesday night, to be precise – I pretended to the man delivering my Thai food that I had a boyfriend, and I also implied that we lived together. I don't like this delivery guy, you see. He's over-familiar. He phones to say he's on the way. Why? Why does he do that? He wants to chat.

On Wednesday, he phoned and said: *Well Maeve, just on the road now – how are you?*

Good – thanks, I replied.

And he replied: *Oh – did I wake you? You sound like you just woke up.*

I was horrified. Why on earth would I take a nap in the time between ordering and having my food delivered? Who does that? I am far too excited about my dinner to snooze. I sit by the window, clutching my phone and counting down the minutes, like everyone else. And importantly, I do not answer the phone to strangers just after I've just woken up: it's too intimate. The only thing I woke up to was the fact that this delivery guy was a goddamn creep. So when he rang the doorbell, I sang out casually, but loudly: *I'll get it, Henry!*

As if I was talking to my live-in lover. My choice of name for this imaginary boyfriend took me by surprise: I only know two Henrys. One is my mother's bulldog, a stinking wreck of a creature. The other is the local undertaker in Cobh, a lovely man – good friend of my Grandad actually.

Baby dressed as sushi

You wouldn't believe the number of times people tell me to stop being such a baby. About once a week, someone comes up with that old chestnut, I swear. I don't get offended. In fact, it pleases me, because babies are the best. In fact, I would actually like to be a baby again, for a few days. Let me be clear, I don't want to be one of those adults that dresses as a baby for kicks, wearing a nappy and holding a giant bottle from the joke shop. That's not what I'm after. You know that song 'Make Someone Happy' that's in every Tom Hanks film from the 1990s? I love the line that goes: *One face that lights when it nears you*. If you're an anyway half-decent baby, most faces will light when they near you.

I cannot help myself from smiling at babies. I pretty much like all babies, from the brand new, kitten-like ones right up to the thumping busters who've seen a thing or two. I like meeting babies and also seeing photos of them and hearing about what they get up to. Sometimes people are a bit apologetic, and say things like: *I'm boring you now, I'm sorry – but here's my niece dressed as Luigi Mario*, and I assure them that they truly are not boring me. Quite the opposite. If they weren't showing me, I'd more than likely be Google-

Imaging exactly that. I'm not alone in this habit. The top ten Google Image suggestions when you type in *baby dressed as* are as follows: baby dressed as turtle; baby dressed as sushi; baby dressed as lobster; baby dressed as old man from *Up*; baby dressed as food; baby dressed as prince; baby dressed as panda; baby dressed as animal; baby dressed as Yoda; baby dressed as doctor.

As much as I love a themed baby, I appreciate babies in casual clothes too. They can't put a chubby foot wrong in a simple white babygro. It's understated and cuddly – a classic baby look.

The only downside to being a massive fan of babies is that I constantly get accused of being broody. I knelt beside my nephew's pram to chat with him in a car park in Midleton one afternoon, and a man pulling out in a van actually shouted at me: *Whoops – someone's broody.* He then waved and drove off, delighted with himself. I don't know how he knew that I wasn't the mother. Maybe because I'm so young and carefree-looking. I didn't get a chance to shout back to him that there's nothing wrong with being broody.

It's lucky some people are broody, because how else could humans continue to exist in this world? If more of us weren't born, think how deserted the place would be. Who would get drunk on reality shows and invent new guns and walk mindlessly around Ikea on a Sunday afternoon?

The thing is, though, Mr I-Drive-a-Van-and-My-Hobby-is-Bullying-Women-Le-Roux, I'm not actually broody. I just really like babies. One of the things a thirty-year-old lady is meant to fret about, if medical science and *Chat* magazine are to be believed, is her baby-making facilities. I've got something like a tonne of a dozen eggs waiting for their special place in Higgins history. As sure as eggs is eggs, I have yet to decide what to do with mine. For ova, they are quite elderly now, though I haven't noticed any difference. They don't seem to mind not being put to use, they're not pranking my phone or sending empty fertiliser bags to the house just yet.

I like babies because they generally do whatever they feel like doing. They are honest about how they feel. If they get bad vibes from a man with a beard, they simply look horrified and cry until he leaves. I need to be more like that. When somebody annoys me or gives me the creeps, I usually just say something under my breath or put the incident into my little store of slights, to think about later. I must take a leaf out of the book of babies, and deal with the irritant promptly and efficiently. By yelling at the person, then crying until they disappear, I bet I would save a lot of time and energy.

My parents say that I had the saddest baby tears in the history of the world. Legend goes, I cried only twice and both times every fox in the neighbourhood ran away and all the swans sank. I cry a lot more as an adult, but the impact is not as dramatic. Probably because the things I cry about are stupid, and also because I usually stop myself from crying before the floods arrive. One day in the gym, my eyes filled up with furious tears because my hips were way too tight for the 16 kg kettlebell, and there was an elderly lady blithely swinging a twenty kg one beside me. But I blinked those hot tears back down, so they don't count. My throat felt thick and my voice went funny recently when I saw a downtrodden middle-aged man unwrap a breakfast roll in his little car; for

201

some reason it made me feel sorry for Ireland – but again, I didn't weep openly. I think that was nice of me, as it would have made him super self-conscious.

It's not *all* wah-wah with babies. There's plenty of ha-ha too. Babies laugh a lot. If someone falls over and makes a funny bleating noise as they do so, babies laugh openly, even if the person is hurt. They are right to, because, despite the end result, the fall and the bleating noise were still very amusing.

When you put a baby in a bath and his eyelashes get wet, they will make his eyes look like stars and you will suddenly realise that everything will be fine.

Who gets woken up to be fed delicious sweet food that they don't even have to chew? Babies do, that's who! And they don't think twice about it. I respect babies for sticking to their guns and not being swayed by trends in the food world. They like pap, and the blander the better. A mashed banana is exotic enough for their honest palates. They shout: *Sorry hipsters, we're sticking to carrot purée! So you can put your sweetbreads back in your copy of* At Swim-Two-Birds, *and cycle off on your BMX.* (Babies aren't really sure what hipsters are up to these days, their jibes are based on one trip to Williamsburg in 2010.)

I admire their magnificent sense of entitlement. Like most of my countrymen, I am obsequious to a fault, forever apologising if someone is in my seat on the train, and thanking waitresses a million. None of that humility for babies – none at all. When you roll on the ground and pretend to be a penguin for twenty minutes for their amusement, don't expect gratitude. You'll be lucky if they smile faintly and demand more.

A game I sometimes play is called *Which Race Has the Best Babies?* It makes some people uncomfortable. They won't play, on the grounds that it's too close to some kind of profiling/racist/stereotyping bone, and also that it suggests judging the babies solely on what they look like. Whatever! It's just a game. It's not like I'm secretly keeping tabs and that's how I'll finally decide who to reproduce with. I mean, seriously, it's not like my ultimate goal is to actually go to the country with the winning ethnicity and steal one of their babies – that would be crazy! I'm laughing here at the very idea of it. Ha-ha-ha! See?

If your interest has been piqued, I will let you know right now who the best babies are. The answer will come as no surprise to those of you who have seen a documentary called *Babies*, or travelled around central Asia. That's right – Mongolian babies are the best babies!

The important thing about all babies is that they are just so bloody cute. They have no muscle tone really, and not much hair, and dribble all over themselves, but the criteria for cuteness is different for them. For example, when your boyfriend farts in the car, you feel a momentary devastation at your poor decision-making skills and your bleak future – whereas it's actually cute and funny when babies fart. Things that a baby needs, like clothes and toys, are also supremely cute. Dresses with pictures of sailboats on them are worn on any old Wednesday afternoon, whether or not there's a party to go to. Bald heads are adorned with pink bows, for no reason other than amping up the adorability of said head. Pop a pair of heart-shaped sunglasses on a baby, or sideways baseball cap, or a helmet shaped like a tiger's head – you just can't go wrong!

Innately lovable toys include wooden tractors and rubber giraffes, and they are things that exist solely for babies to stare at, grab and chew on. How ugly the world would be if it was full of just adult things. A laptop and a wine bottle don't hold a candle to a plastic piano and an octopus made of green felt.

Babies don't care what they look like, as evidenced by the wild hairstyles many of them adopt. Their version of bedhead, with curls sticking to a sweaty forehead and cheeks burning red, is the loveliest thing you'll see all day. I also like the 'Mafia Don' style – a ring of fine hair all around a pudgy bald spot at the back. There's also the increasingly popular 'just curls' look, a reaction against their straightener-crazed forebears. That said, a number of babies stick to the traditional 'single vertical fountain' for girls or the 'Sterling Cooper Draper Pryce side parting' for boys.

Unlike large children or adults, you can pick babies up and carry them around: they are such a handy size. The stuff that comes with babies is also miniature, and that adds to the fun. Who hasn't enjoyed holding up an adult pair of dungarees next to a baby pair? Who doesn't long to see a tiny Irish breakfast made with cocktail sausages, cherry tomatoes and a fried quail's egg? We all love to see small versions of things, and babies create a whole wonderful industry of tininess around themselves.

Spend ten minutes watching a baby lie on a rug, holding his toes and humming to himself, and you can shake off that long-held suspicion that you are a cyborg incapable of being floored by something like absolute love.

When a baby disapproves of you, it feels terrible. This is for a reason. Don't shrug it off and think: *That dumbo baby doesn't have a clue! I'm a bloody legend!* You're not a bloody legend – stop fooling yourself. Babies are truth-seers. If they dislike you, there must be a stain on your character. Go back over your life. Dig up your most painful mistakes from the past and try to right them. Did you kick a dog in the face when nobody was around, because he was making gross mouth sounds? Apologise to him now and never do it again. Perhaps you lied in the emergency room about eating an entire pavlova and acted like you didn't know what was wrong with you? If so, make amends by only ever eating a couple of slices of pavlova in one sitting from now on. Did you steal a block of photocopying paper from Ireland's state broadcaster? That's fine: they didn't recommission your TV show, even though it was really good. They said to your friend that it was too niche and that's how you found out it was cancelled – so you should totally help yourself to photocopying paper, babies won't hold that against you. You'll have to look closer to figure out what changes you can make to your personality, attitude or appearance to gain their approval. It will be worth it, because listen to me kid, in this crazy old world? There is no sweeter feeling than a baby thinking you're alright.

The opening scenes of three blockbuster romantic comedies starring me

1. I am a supple gymnast and it is wartime. I am getting my teeth cleaned one afternoon, when suddenly my village gets completely massacred – absolutely everyone is killed! (When you see this in the cinema, you will be taken aback. I plan to make the killing quite confronting, but don't worry – the romance and the comedy are just around the corner!)

A man from a peacekeeping mission comes to interview me. It is all quite stark and professional, and his questions are along the lines of: *Who do you think did this, like?* In a very human moment, I get tearful when I talk about everyone I know – except my dental hygienist – being murdered. The man hugs me to make me feel better and I notice how ripped he is under his bullet-proof vest. This guy is cut, seriously. Body fat around 8 per cent: unreal definition. Big, not bulky – great proportions. A lot of strength training has gone into this powerful physique, that's for sure. An OK face.

After the interview, I move to a new place and begin the difficult task of setting up a new life. I gradually replace my previous social structures – I join another library, I set up a pot-luck night, and so on. Then it happens again!

206

Another massacre. (This is the comedy part – it's like, what an unlucky girl!) There follows a number of atrocities, in which I somehow manage to avoid getting killed. It just keeps happening. The in-great-shape human rights guy is sent to investigate each incident, and there I am. He initially suspects me of being a war criminal, but gradually falls in love with me.

2. I am a clever physicist getting my teeth cleaned. I have left my bike outside the hygienist's office, locked to a lamp post that already had one bike attached to it. Because I was so focused on my career and distracted by an experiment back at the lab, I have accidentally locked the bikes together. After my appointment (which goes really well), I go to get my bike and the owner of the other bike is standing there, trying to figure out how to get his free. He smiles and I notice he has just had his teeth cleaned too. (A number of hygienists work out of the same building – this will be established in the opening shots.)

I search and search my bag but I can't find the key for my bike lock. The other bike owner is massively irritated by this. He punches the lamppost, and I notice how strong he is. The power in the punch is fuelled by rage but also, I suspect, by years of mixed martial arts training. Impressively explosive, I have to say, like eighty per cent fast-twitch muscle fibre or something, I bet! He has sort of black hair. I tell him I must have left my keys in the hygienist's office. He calms down a bit and says, *You get your teeth cleaned by Ms Phelan too?* I explain that I have been treated by Ms Phelan occasionally, but my regular hygienist is her colleague, Ms Trent, just down the corridor. He says Ms Trent is good too: she advised him about his gingivitis when Ms Phelan was on maternity leave last year. He got it under control before it got anywhere close to periodontal disease, and we laugh about this. He realises all the coincidences are caused by fate bringing us together and becomes gradually more smitten.

3. I am a sallow cellist on holiday in Seville. I've just popped in to the local dental hygienist for a quick polish, when I realise I've left my wallet on the kitchen counter-top in Dublin 8. I go ahead and get my teeth cleaned anyway, all the while trying to figure out how to pay for it. The hygienist is concerned about a spot on one of my second premolars and orders an X-ray. I find that refreshing, as in Ireland, hygienists aren't usually so proactive. (I will say that in a voiceover – I'm not afraid to make statements like that in my work, even if they cause ripples back home.)

Anyway, the X-ray man comes in and gives me a plate to bite down on, and as he does so, I notice he has a powerfully athletic build. Like he played rugby for years, but realised what it was doing to his personality, so stopped, but kept up the training. Importantly, his shoulders and pecs are extraordinarily symmetrical. By accident, I swallow too much mouth rinse and go unconscious.

When I come to, he is in the process of falling for me,

hard – because his thing is unconscious women, and I look so cute when I'm passed out. Because of the obvious chemistry between myself and 'El Radiógrafo', the hygienist does not charge me for the cleaning OR the X-ray.

My hair, my journey: a chronological account

0–3 years: I was born with a head of thick black hair. My mother said her hair got thinner after she had each one of us, and our hair got thicker. I was third out, so I know I have Grade 3 hair. When it grew, it grew curly. Soft, shiny, black curls – like Phil Lynott had. Everyone knew I was a baby girl because of my beautiful hair, and high heels.

4–8 years: My hair straightened itself mysteriously. My curls fled in the night and I was left with a secretary's bob. Nice and tidy, tucked behind my ears when I was working on something. In my downtime, it was free to just frame my incredibly round face.

9–10 years: Short hair, high on top for me at this point. I do not remember making the decision to get all of my hair cut off. The family weren't lice-infested for another four years, yet I had very short hair. Not dramatically short, not like a 1950s prisoner of war. More like a former prisoner of war, back home in Indianapolis, who has put all of that behind him and now lives in a nice house with a picket fence, sells insurance in the city and keeps his hair clipped tidily.

11–14 years: Things started to get confusing for my hair. The curls came stealing back in, but their heart was just not in it. They were gone for too long, and all had changed. Where there once was softness, there was now wire. Where there once was an ebony shine, there was now just plain dull. I decided the most practical 'do would be an undercut. The barber suggested tapering my hair down to the centre of my neck instead, worried that an undercut would be too harsh. I reiterated how I wanted it to *feel lighter and shaved off* – so he removed a two-inch section and I left the rest hang slightly over it. From the front, it was an almost perfect triangle around my face. I styled it by wetting my fingers under the tap and pulling the frizziest parts out around my forehead. The water shaped the frizz into small, tight curls. In the school bathroom one day, a girl with long blonde hair and icy eyes made me show her how I did it. I couldn't read her expression, as I explained to her how easy it was and consoled her for not being able to do the same thing with her hair. It was a smile, of sorts. Almost like an *absolutely dying to tell everybody about what a retard Maeve is* smile – but I couldn't be sure.

15–18 years: These were the middle-crease/low-bun years. I grew my hair long. You would never have known that, because I wore it scraped down flat on either side of my head and wound tightly into a bun that lived all day in the nape of my neck. I needed serious hair for babysitting and for sustained letter-writing campaigns directed at various dictators, demanding that they change their ways.

19–22 years: I went back to the bob. It's a classic for a reason, you know. This time around, I didn't want my own bob, though. I wanted Meg Ryan's. *Choppy* was the word whirling around and around my mind. I had it on a constant loop, humming to the tune of Robin Hood. *Choppy bob, choppy bob, walking up the stairs. Choppy bob, choppy bob, sitting on some chairs.* The hairdresser was unable to deliver. Instead of a witch using her dark art to transplant Meg Ryan's head onto my neck, I got a nervous trainee with a scissors who didn't know that curls get shorter – much, much shorter – as they dry.

23 years: I had dreadlocks. Maybe it seems like I am just making that up to impress you, because dreadlocks are such a cool hairstyle on a white person. Maybe you don't believe that I had dreadlocks. Well, I did. And I don't mean ones that were attached to the back of a beanie hat as part of a hilarious fancy-dress outfit. They were real, and very difficult to achieve.

I was working in a gift shop in Cobh for a summer, selling lamps made out of bog wood to tourists. Don't get me wrong – I loved it – but something was missing. I did a lot of research online and then talked to all of the African hairdressers working in Cork city. One told me that she couldn't do it. Her words, kindly said, were: *No way, it is not fair for you.* The other said she could, that it would be no problem – but it would be expensive. How much? She sucked her teeth and came up with a figure that just happened to be the exact same as what I was earning each week in the gift shop. I didn't call that expensive. I called that a small price to pay to nice up my head. So I went back the following week, paid her upfront, then sat in the chair as she rubbed Dax Wax into my hair, then split it into sections and twirled it around loosely with her fingers. I sensed that the dreads wouldn't take, but didn't want to be culturally insensitive, so thanked her politely and left the salon, her warnings not to wash my hair for three days ringing in my ears. The next morning my hair was a solid, white mass of wax, with no discernible dreadlocks. I had to wash it with almost boiling water every day for the rest of the week. Two months later, back in Dublin, my best friend Ian sat on the sofa and I sat between his knees on the ground. Then he went to work, knotting each strand of hair into a knobbly little lock with the needle. There we stayed for hours, watching re-runs of *Murder She Wrote* and eating Maltesers, as is tradition in Trench Town. I wasn't worried about how wispy and thin my dreads were in the beginning, because it's like I always say: the child must creep before him walk.

23½ years: I cut my dreads off myself, quite late one night. I don't think it's fair how films always show someone cutting their hair off as a prelude to them going 100 per cent bonkers. I was fine! I noticed a lot of greys coming through, and I felt a bit sad, but mentally stable. Most of my family go grey young, because we are so elegant and hard-working. Thus began my relationship with hair colour. I am seduced by words like chestnut and chocolate, because they are delicious foods. So I ask the colourist for chocolate and chestnut hair, and that is how I get my signature 'brown-haired woman' look.

28 years: For almost a year, I tried really hard to be a redhead. What I wanted and needed to do was to lose weight, but I decided to focus first on getting my hair the right shade of sassy auburn. I had it stripped – which is a process that removes the natural colour and leaves your hair a dull peach hue. Then I had it dyed deep orange. I was not happy with it because, like I said, what I really wanted and needed to do was lose weight. I went back and had it dyed medium orange. And so on.

29 years to present: One great thing about having a scatter of sisters who look like me is that I can see how they wear their hair and mimic them. I mean, really mimic them – down to the way they hold their cutlery. They complain about the way I study them, but it is my right as a relative to do so.

My younger sister Daisy always looks great and she changes her hair all the time, like one of those mannequin heads that hairdressers learn on. Though she is far more animate and sometimes wears glasses, which those heads never do. I have noted that a side fringe remains a regular feature of each style she adopts. I see that it suits our face shape. So I have a side fringe too. I sometimes blow-dry the rest of my hair so it's shiny and big, like an American mom's. I often plait it and pin the plaits along the top of my head, like a German grandmother. I get a lot of compliments for that, actually. Once a young comedian crossed a room to tell me it was the best way he'd seen my hair done. I've liked him ever since. Sometimes I leave it dry naturally and pin it up like a Jane Austen character – in a hoody, I don't leave it down unless

I'm going to bed or need to do a quick impersonation of an Irish folk singer.

So, now you know some of the twists and turns of my hair through the years. I'm still learning, so don't look to me for all your hair-related questions. I would say this: treat your hairdresser well, and she will treat you well and not play any mean tricks on you. Once, I was impatient with my hairdresser. She asked me how I wanted my hair blow-dried and I said: *Oh, it doesn't matter – whatever way is fastest.* I regretted saying that as I watched her face fall – in eleven different mirrors. I realised that, not only had I belittled her profession and implied she was taking too long, but I'd ruined my chance of a bouncy blow-dry that would last three days. I said I was sorry and she said: *Don't worry about it*, but I knew I'd hurt her feelings. I thought about trying to compensate with an extra-large tip, but thought that might be patronising. So I didn't tip her at all.

Tricked you! Of course I tipped her. And just the right amount: not too much and not too little. I fancy myself as the Goldilocks of tipping, or rather, the child-bear's porridge in the story of Goldilocks of tipping.

In my defence, I had gotten my colour and cut done on the same day (a classic boom time move), so had been sitting in the chair for over two hours, and my back was sore. Did I ever tell you that I slipped a disc one time? Well, if I did, I lied. I didn't slip a disc – but one bulged. I hate to think of it, bulging away in between my vertebrae. I don't like the word 'bulge'. So I just say it slipped, even though that is a far worse condition. This fib does mean I occasionally get undue sympathy from people. To be honest with you, I enjoy it. Lock me up and throw away the key, why don't you? I got to get my jollies somehow. And it balances out all the times I've started telling someone: *So, I hurt my back . . .* and all it does is trigger their story about how *they* hurt *their* back.

There was more to it than just a sore back that time, though. While in the chair, I had looked at so many celebrity magazines, I felt sick. Not physically: more nauseous in my essence, my being, my soul, or whatever you call that important part of a person that should remain intact at all times, but doesn't because of celebrity magazines. That's why I was a dickhead to the hairdresser, and I regret it.

Since then, whenever I go to the hairdressers, I am careful to <u>avoid</u> a number of things and I urge you to do the same. These are:

- Celebrity magazines.

- The biscuit that comes with the tea. Gluten sensitive, remember?

- Looking at the time. This prevents feelings of guilt. I don't have an important life or a demanding schedule, yet I can't shake the feeling that primping time is shamefully self-indulgent. Even the fact that I call getting a haircut 'primping time' proves I belong somewhere in Roscommon in the 1950s, getting Churched or whatever.

–   Looking in the mirror. It does nobody any good
to see themselves when their body is draped in a
black sheet and their head is tiny and wet. Like a
bald eagle, without the pride.

The sad, short life of Pip the calf

As a bookish, lazy, cake-making sort of a woman, I am very surprised at my new hobby, which is moving my body around doing a thing called exercise. It started over a year ago, with running. Lots of women, when they're running across the road, do a sort of embarrassed half-laugh, as if to say: *Isn't it silly? Me, running?* I felt like that. I used to not run for the bus in case I missed it. What an upbeat, logical little creature I was! It got to the point where I began to deliberately slow my walking pace down, so the driver wouldn't think I wanted to board the bus at all. I even waved him on once, before settling down on the bench for a forty-minute wait, just to avoid the potential embarrassment of strangers seeing me try and fail at something.

These days, I run for buses. Sometimes when they're not even my bus. Let me tell you this: if I run for, and make it onto, a bus you're sitting on, I will gaze at you expectantly, panting, until we have a short chat, where I can relive the glory of what just happened and you can congratulate me for my efforts. That kind of thing – a short burst of physical activity, followed by warm praise from a stranger – really sets me up for the day.

My sister Raedi is a running coach and, as you know, we live together. Raedi is super-fit. She runs up mountains and lifts heavy weights. Her hair is like shimmering ropes and she has nails like diamonds. I must have decided somewhere along the way that being organised and fit was her department, and that being chaotic and fat was mine, because that's how things played out for a long time. My logic was flawed. For one thing, Raedi wasn't always super-fit. She started running after a particularly indulgent summer spent working in a multiplex cinema in Hawaii, where the tubs of ice cream were as big as the sun and the butter flowed like lava over popcorn mountains. She returned home very brown and very round – more Hawaiian than the Hawaiians themselves.

Raedi took herself in hand and began running – early in the morning, so nobody would see her. Me and the rest of the family were concerned. When she returned home, sweating, we'd get her a chair and a glass of water. *But your face is so red,* we'd say … *and your heart is racing!* bewildered as to how this could possibly be healthy. I think we had outdated notions of women and exercise, from watching *Pride and Prejudice* hundreds of times. When Raedi started to shift her gift, our instinct was to crowd around her and fan her with our bonnets, saying things like: *Someone, fetch the carriage at once – the young lady is quite spent, and mustn't exert herself further or she may take a turn!*

I followed her progress over the years with some interest. In between popping Maltesers into my mouth, I shouted encouraging things to her, as she ran, swam and cycled in various triathlons. I was proud of her, but confused about what it meant for me, especially when other members of the family began joining in with this whole exercise thing.

My father and my brother got road bikes that you click your feet into, thereby becoming half men, half racer bikes. Rosie started kickboxing and running half marathons and almost immediately got a six-pack. Daisy started salsa dancing and almost immediately got a foreign boyfriend. Ettie brought DVDs back with her to Somalia, with terrifying titles like *Shred Yourself, You Sexy Bitch* and *Punch, Kick, Just Never Stop Pumpin' – Cardio 'til You Die*. That's how she became the wiry little humanitarian street fighter we are all scared of today.

I didn't like that Raedi was always willing me, gently, to make an effort to be healthy, and I resisted for a long time. Finally, after my ticker started acting up with the old Graves' and I felt like the most wretched girl in the history of the world, I had to give it a try. Once I'd made the decision, I thought the rest would fall into place. In the film of my life, there followed a montage including the following scenes:

– Me doing hundreds of those push-ups where you clap between each one, but instead of one clap, I do long rounds of applause because my core is ridiculously tight.

– Me winning the Tour de France and holding both arms aloft as I cross the finishing line, because not only am I a fast and tenacious cyclist, I am also co-ordinated enough not to fall off when I go 'sans hands'.

- Me in a cage wrestling a Great Dane and him trying desperately to tap out.

- Me teaching lots of old Chinese men how to do martial arts. At break time, they whisper reverently about how focused and disciplined I am and I both hear and understand what they are saying, as my senses are sharpened by all the training and I speak Mandarin.

- Me punching Mike Tyson incredibly hard, again and again, until the ref stops the fight. Me getting the same tattoo as Mike Tyson – the tribal one around his left eye. It looks way better on me, thereby I doubly humiliate him.

To date, not even one of those situations has come to pass. Getting fit takes a while and there are loads of different ways to do it. You don't need me to tell *you* that, Michael Fassbender. Anyway, what I have figured out, at the age of thirty, is that my body is made to move. After years spent carefully guarding it against activity and saying things like – *Oh thank God, there's a lift* and *I'll just wait here until the tide goes out again* – I now do all sorts of activities, like running, weight-lifting, and pilates. I also sometimes take boxing classes, so if you see me sauntering around your neighbourhood, you'd better keep your wits about you and your dukes up.

Rest assured, those of you who, sweetly, worry about me sounding like a show-off, I do all of these things quite badly. But the more I move around, the better I feel. About everything. IT'S TOTALLY BRILLIANT! DO YOU HEAR ME? IT'S THE GREATEST!! Lots of people must already know that. Why else would sport be popular? It just never occurred to me before. I've slowly figured out that people with gym bags must play football after work and people who carry yoga mats around probably do yoga. And people who eat chicken salad for lunch, when they could have cake, are not psychopath-freakazoids – they are just taking care of themselves.

As a chubby teenager with low self-esteem, giant braces and even bigger glasses, I would daydream about leaving Cobh and returning transformed, like a beautiful swan. Not an actual swan, but a thin girl with straight teeth, straight eyes and inner calm. Old people would walk off the pier with distraction; men would weep in amazement; toddlers would drop their ice creams in awe. I'd wave, and say in a gentle voice: *It is I, Maeve, come back to you – an absolute rocket, and therefore a better person.*

I know better than that now. I no longer want to radically alter myself. I just want to keep Momma nice. And, mainly, I want to be strong. Considering that I used to struggle with full teapots, I've already come a long way. For example, I was recently rushing out of Lidl on Thomas Street in Dublin with a heavy box of shopping, when I spotted a huge puddle of vomit on the ground outside the €2 shop. I was almost upon it, so had to jump over it quickly, while holding onto the box. It was no problem to me! That's called functional fitness, when you can make a depressing, real-life situation a bit less bleak for yourself by being in OK shape.

I'd love to be super-strong. Like my trainer, Seán. He is so strong! The things he can lift up and put back down again, aye yi yi!! He is the boss of his body and that is so great! I want to call him 'Coach' and have him call me 'Champ', but I am too self-conscious to ask.

I have a lot of wildly different feelings when I'm in the gym. I like the other people there because we chat about our fitness goals, whereas my friends from my other life – the one involving sitting and cakes – don't like it when I go on about how cool it would be to do a chin-up. I love days when I can do something I wasn't able to do the previous week. I also like having a shower at the gym because the shower there is much better than my shower at home. The water pressure in the bathroom at home is so low, it's like the water is apologising in whispers all around my body. It gives me the creeps.

I try to think strong in the gym, and not get scared of things that are difficult or uncomfortable. Some days, though, when it gets really hard and my confidence doesn't hold up, I get a chant playing on a loop in my head. It goes: *I'm allergic to this, I'm allergic to this, I'm allergic to this.* Then I don't know what to do with myself, apart from take a deep breath and try not to cry. Another thing is that, even when a workout is physically challenging, it can sometimes also be boring. Once a cat walked past the doorway and I was thrilled, because it gave me something to think about for nearly my whole last set of rows.

In the gym, there's often a man telling you what to do and putting his hands on you, and it may go against your instincts to actually pay for that. It's OK, though, he's just a trainer and he is just training you. Another thing I've noticed is that everything is metal or plastic, there's no aged wood or willow pattern china or cushions covered in floral fabric, like in the other places I spend time in. And the main thing to remember is that you really have to focus, you can't get distracted by a noise or an idea, or you could injure yourself. Say a cat walks past the door of the gym and you lose yourself in thoughts of where he could be off to – in the middle of an industrial estate, of all places! Was he dumped because of the recession? Was he just curious about car showrooms? You get lost in one cat's story and you just might get your fingers jammed under the 22.5 kg dumbbells – and that really hurts.

I still do it, though, because it makes me strong, and also has made my body sort of change shape. Not in a paranormal shape-shifter way, I can't slip under doors or fit into bathroom cabinets … yet. But since I started moving around the place quickly and picking up heavy things, my clothes fit me better. Not to the point of me standing in one pant leg of a clown's trousers and holding out the other leg, making a funny face – they just fit better. It's like, where I used to have absolutely no bottom, I now have one.

Can you understand what I'm telling you? Let me explain. A couple of years ago, I was home for the weekend and we were all sitting around the kitchen table. You know, me and my sisters, up to our usual tricks: snacking and verbally eviscerating people. My mother was stacking the dishwasher and the rest of us were laughing because she has no bottom. As she bent over doing her work, she made an exact right angle. Then Rosie said to me: *I don't know what you're laughing at, Maeve – you've got the exact same non-bottom!*

I was shocked but couldn't deny it, as I had never seen back there for myself. My head doesn't go fully around to the back, you see, it always gets stuck just at my shoulder. Helpfully, Rosie spent that afternoon setting up a hall of mirrors so that I'd see my behind from all angles. It was devastating.

The truth, tragically, was that, like my mother before me, my legs went straight up into my back. I had no bottom. I was bottomless. I should clarify that I've always had a functioning bottom. Everything downstairs works just fine. Oh, listen to me, boasting! I just didn't have the *shape* of one. There was no external manifestation of a bottom. In the fruit bowl of life, if some women are pears and some are apples, then myself and my mother were a pair of crêpes, without any fruit filling.*

I never wore jeans. Me, famously down to earth and 'one of the people', yet I could not wear these common trousers. The problem with jeans is that they all come with an in-built section at the top, where your bottom is supposed to go. When I tried to wear them, that space was empty and just hung there. It was very sad, like when you set a place for somebody at Christmas dinner and only then remember that they died during the year. It's realising the absence that's the hardest.

I wear jeans now, though, let me tell you, and there is positively no sagging. I bet I could even wear dungarees, for crying out loud! I will tell you how I got my butt, the one that

---

* I realise crêpes are not a fruit, but cannot think of any flat fruit. Somebody needs to invent new fruits to cater for the increasing need for metaphors as body shapes change over time. Call the President!

just doesn't quit. But I must first tell you about a calf from Cobh I met once that had no butt whatsoever. Under his tail, there was just a smooth surface. We went on a school walk to see him.

In case you don't know, school walks are different to school tours. There were only two teachers and eighty children in our school, so sometimes the teachers would get sick of us and send us, unaccompanied, on a school walk. Once we walked four miles to see some daffodils. A girl in fifth class told us that they are used in salads in France. The dope was mixing up daffodils with nasturtiums, of course! We took her word for it, though, and ate a couple of flowers each. Soon afterwards, we began to throw up – in an unforgettably vivid way. A more successful school walk was when we went to the strand to collect any 'unusual stones', and one boy found a stone shaped sort of like an egg.

This time, with the calf, we had high hopes of seeing something really cool, so we walked as fast as we could to the farm, about half a mile from the school. We queued up outside the shed and went in one by one: I think we did this individually to heighten the suspense. I was third in because I was third biggest in the school (including the boys).

I walked into the dark shed and the farmer nodded to me in that slight way they nod, then he held the calf's tail aloft and I saw that it was true: the little fellow had no asshole. When everyone had filed back out of the shed, we took the small ones' hands and walked back to school.

The farmer rang a few hours later. We were in the middle of a class discussion on holy water. I beg your pardon, Holy Water. The teacher was advising us to tell any of our parents that wore contact lenses to soak them overnight in Holy Water, as this would prevent them from crashing their cars. She briefly stopped teaching magical thinking to take the phone call, and then passed on to us the message that the calf had died. One girl started crying, but nobody else joined in. On the walk back, some of us had discussed the possibility of the calf dying, so we weren't surprised. It was inevitable: without surgical action to fix as big a physiological issue of having no bottom, anyone would die.

I don't know what happened to the little, bottomless carcass. Abattoirs don't accept already dead animals, in case they pass on some disease to the most important creatures of all: humans. If you find a dead animal, don't even bother bringing it to an abattoir – they won't take it. Even if you put a hat and sunglasses on it and tape it to your leg and insist: *It's fine, look at it walking alongside me.* Be that as it may, I watched carefully that spring as the farmer's children steadily grew stronger nails and shinier hair – the unmistakable shine one can only get from a freezer full of home-grown protein. So that's the sad, short life of Pip the calf.

Speaking of protein, I believe it played a part in me finally achieving a bottom. I used to eat toast – or bread heated up by the toaster but not quite toast, because I couldn't wait that long – but now I eat eggs and turkey and salmon. Strength training also helped me to achieve my modest dream of glutes to call my own. Whatever went down, I can tell you right now that when I walk into a room, particularly backwards, guys be all like, *Watch out! Mmmaeve's in the building!*

Getting in shape has led to other pleasant surprises too. Since I've started running, it's easier to take Raedi's new dog to the park. She is a Doberman crossed with something very thin. She has a broad, muscular body, with a tiny, narrow head – it's very unfortunate. Because I lack authority and Penny is very naughty, she runs away from me constantly and I have to chase her to get her back on the lead. She sort of smiles as she zooms away from me again and again. It is humiliating to realise just how much a puppy is in charge of me, but it's cool that I don't get out of breath, even after twenty-five minutes of chasing and beseeching. It's kind of like how Beyoncé can sing and dance at the same time.

Also, I used to be uptight about getting close to strangers but now, in yoga class, strangers' groins sometimes get breathtakingly near my face – and it's totally fine! I've discovered that where I used to be precious about not feeling too warm, I now like the feeling of really, really needing a shower. Similarly (and carrying the same bourgeoisie alert), I love being physically exhausted at the end of the day. Maybe I should be in a war, or have a baby: from what I've heard, those events induce a similar reaction. For now, though, I'll just keep running after the anvil-headed dog and picking up actual anvils when my trainer tells me to. And possibly, I'll start referring to myself, quietly, as 'Champ'.

So much happens on the inside

*A*sk anyone at all and they'll tell you: my pelvic floor is super-tight. That's the kind of statement I was hoping to be able to make right after my first Pilates class two years ago. I didn't realise a couple of things:

- It takes a while to figure out where your pelvic floor actually is.

- You can't really tell from the outside whether or not someone has a super-tight pelvic floor, unless they are doing some kind of public show about it.

Oh, and I hadn't expected that at times, Pilates feels like a sex class, but not in a sexy way. More like 'going through a series of moves from a particularly mechanical sex manual' way, specifically when the teacher tells you to squeeze, lift and then zip up your jeans. Luckily, that distracting idea darted away quickly when we went on to the Bridge and the Hundred, and all I could think about was trying to stay as steady as the girl beside me.

That was one curious thing about the class I joined in my local community centre: it was all women. I didn't think too much about it. Although I'm not exactly a doctor, I am a woman, and can say with complete authority that it's important for women to take care of their pelvic floors. Pilates helps you to do that, as do Kegel exercises.

Top tip: a fun thing to do when you're out on the town with your girlfriends is to guess when they're doing their Kegels. I do that, and it's easy. We'll be sitting in a pub and they'll be telling everyone about the book they're reading, and suddenly I'll cut across them. *Now?* I shout. *Are you doing them now?* If I've guessed right, they have to buy me a small bag of dry roasted peanuts as a reward. Another ideal spot is in the cinema – I simply lean across and whisper: *Are you Kegeling right now?* If their answer is: *Stop being such a creep, Maeve,* I sit back, disappointed in them, and do not offer them any more Minstrels.

So, back to my first Pilates class. The teacher made a short speech in the beginning, about how we were going to reclaim our bodies, build up a strong core once more, and take this one hour a week for ourselves and ourselves alone. She had me at 'reclaim'. I bloody love when women talk like that.

The first few weeks were tricky. I realised early on that, because so much happens on the inside, I could get away with lying on the mat and kind of doing nothing, except maybe just the breathing part. Then I manned up, really applied myself and started to figure it out. At the end of the first six weeks, our teacher said: *OK everyone – next week, bring your small ones: it's a Mammy-and-me class.* I scoffed and looked around, but everybody was nodding and rolling up their mats as if there was nothing strange about her assuming we all had babies. That's when I figured out that it was a Pilates class for new mothers, more specifically, as the woman in charge of the community centre later told me, *a Dublin City Council class for unmarried mothers.*

It suddenly made sense that everyone looked so tired! It also explained the empowering speech at the start, and one of my classmate's neck tattoos that read: *Only God Can Judge Me.* I loved the class, so kept schtum and spent the next day phoning around friends and family to see if they had a reasonably toned baby (preferably with dark curly hair and a side fringe) that I could borrow, just for an hour. I'm a smart cookie, see? A smart cookie with, at this stage, a reasonably tight pelvic floor.

Sometimes, late at night, I lie awake and watch you sleeping

You know how in Garth Brooks' song 'Unanswered Prayers', he sings: *Sometimes, late at night, I lie awake and watch you sleeping, you're lost in peaceful dreams, so I turn out the light and lay there in the dark*? A beautiful image there – him lying in the dark. Well, do you know that song? You must. I know the words to many Garth Brooks songs, though not deliberately. His lyrics have just seeped into me by osmosis – like rumours about sugar somehow not being good for me.

I am on the hostile side of ambivalent when it comes to country music. I did love when Brooks dyed his hair and changed his name for a brief, mad moment, and everybody played along and said, at the end of his concerts: *Well done, Chris.* Anyway, here is why I'm bringing it up. Sometimes, late at night, I lie awake and think about what a loser I am. Principally because, five years ago, I bought a car but never drove it, and in the end there was an animal living in it and then it got stolen.

I bought a car because I really needed to drive to gigs. Being a stand-up comedian involves going quite far out of your way to the towns where a few people that like your style live, and doing a show especially for them. You can't expect people to come to you, unless you've been on TV for ages doing a lot of middle-of-the-road material and they are zombie-sheep. I reckoned owning a car would surely force me to drive and that way I could avoid the hassle of finding another comedian to drive and do support. That is tricky because most of the ones who can drive are slightly better than me at the old comedy, and a show is never fun when the opening act has blown you out of the water – the water being made of giggles. However, the double pillars of procrastination – being scared and being lazy – prevented me from ever getting into that damn car.

It sat outside my house until I grew too ashamed to pass it every day. I begged my friend Maria to put it in her underground car park. There it languished for eighteen months, until Maria phoned me to say there was something living in it and all the windows were broken. I phoned a towing company and arranged to meet them at the car park. When I arrived, I couldn't see the car anywhere. I knew it was a wine colour and was inhabited by a creature, but I still couldn't find it. The tow truck man said it must have been robbed, but he still needed €35 as a call-out fee. I gave him €twenty and he seemed pleased. Then I went to the police and sang like a canary.

I told them the whole story, even though they just needed the registration number. I emphasised to the perplexed gardai that I will learn to drive one day: I must. It maddens me to think of all the different types of people I know who can drive. Dopey people, mean-spirited people, hop heads, lowdown dirty rats – all having a ball in their cars, and here's me, static. I accept that it's my fault but also blame my three driving instructors. For various reasons, they've put me off: off the road and also off my path to being Miss Independent. The three unhelpful Graces, in chronological order, are as follows:

1. We grew up in a rural spot, so whenever we needed to go anywhere, my parents had to drive us. They were lucky with me – trips to the orthodontist and the optician every few months were my only social outlets. My hobbies were listening to music in my room while feeling furious, or going for walks around the fields while feeling furious – neither of which required getting a lift. I was given six driving lessons as a seventeenth-birthday present.

    I wasn't scared of the car but I was scared of the instructor. His name was Dick Michaels and that's what it said on top of the car: *Dick Michaels' School of Driving*. He was very nice and patient with me, until we were driving up a hill and some boys walking on the footpath yelled: *Dick Michaels SUCKS dick!* I looked at him but he seemed not to have heard. Then he told me to pull in, so I did. He jumped out of the car, ran after the boys and slammed one of them against a wall. He yelled at him for a bit until the boy wriggled free and ran away, openly weeping. Then Dick got back into the passenger seat and said, with just a smidgeon of residual rage: *Now we'll try a hill start.* I couldn't,

I was too busy looking at the veins in his neck and wondering if they were going to burst.

2. I tried driving again when I first moved to Dublin. My instructor was called Saad. He asked me if I liked American movies, and I said I liked some of them. He was frustrated by my answer and refused to speak to me again, apart from the most rudimentary of instructions. I worked on Saad for weeks. *I like* Die Hard – I'd say, hopefully, or: Maid in Manhattan *wasn't that bad.* But he would just sigh and look at his phone.

3. Last year I took one lesson from a middle-aged man who farted quietly and wickedly through the entire hour. As my brother's Mongolian ex-girlfriend would exclaim when people did rotten things: *Oh, how to live?!*

When I do get wheels again, and actually figure out how to use them, I am confident that I will be a great driver. People will get turned on as I drive past, because I'll drive so safely and at exactly the speed limit. I will check my mirrors and change gears and not throw rubbish out the window. I will know whether my car is diesel or petrol, and write it on my hand so as not to forget. I will pass my driving test first time around, and sing 'Friends In Low Places' all the way home.

My two-pronged approach to getting somewhere over the rainbow

1 Invent and manufacture 'The Garment'

'The Garment' is a piece of clothing that has multiple functions. By that, I don't mean like when it's the first cold snap of the winter, and I wear socks on my hands for cycling. Neither do I mean wrapping a jumper around your head and securing it with a brooch, like Little Edie Beale. She looked great, but unfortunately we are not all ruined heiresses living with our mothers.

This is the slogan, which would be used for a multi-platform advertising campaign:

If you are going on a business trip or a weekend away, a wedding or a doctor's appointment, The Garment will do the trick – just pop it into a plastic bag and off you go – no need for a suitcase!

It's not catchy, but it does a great job of explaining what I mean. The Garment is simple and black and doesn't crease. It is all you need, clothing-wise. It has to be simple, because I have learned that to be taken seriously you cannot have any feathers or pictures of zebras on your person. It must be black, because black is the colour of coffee and coffee means

SUCCESS. Also, these days you never know when you'll need to attend a funeral or sit in a bus station for a couple of hours, reading your book. Both of these situations call for clothes with a sombre tone. You'll thank me for this tip. If you're dressed brightly at a funeral, it seems like you don't grasp the finality of death, and if you're dressed brightly at a bus station, all manner of lunatics will flock to you.

The Garment mustn't crease. I have learned this from my calling as a comedian. We fall largely into two categories. The first wear shirts and suits. I think they look untrustworthy, like marketing guys. The second – my category – wears rumpled old clothes that give the impression we are just regular folk: nothing fancy, nothing grand. This is to better bond with our downtrodden, proletariat audiences. It also comes from a deep laziness that is intrinsic to our natures. In 2008, I made a rule for myself that I would not go onstage with any food stains on my clothes, no matter how invisible I thought they seemed. Now, with The Garment, I am taking it one step further and will never look dishevelled again.

When technology catches up with my plans, The Garment will be available in chain mail too, for style and practicality purposes. I will eventually expand to the lucrative children's clothing market and create Le Bébé Garment, nappy included, for the busy baby. For now, though, what looks like a long piece of fabric can become whatever you desire, depending on which way you fold it. Tuck it up in a certain jaunty fold if you find yourself on a trawler – it makes a cute fisherman's hat. Roll it around your midriff, to create an apron for a confectionery emergency. Hang it off your shoulders, to create an elegant, frightening cape. Or transform yourself into an ultra-feminine, ultra-tough executive, by wearing The Garment as a power suit, with power shoulder pads and power bra inserts. The Garment will take you from the bedroom to the boardroom to the ballroom and back again, with the toilet stops, stair climbs and train trips in between.

2. Create the Ultimate Stationery Box

One day I will get my hands on a big metal box and it will be my stationery box. I will go to some kind of outlet store and buy everything I need for the rest of my life, office supplies-wise. I will get a label-maker, a thousand tiny paper rings, coloured pencils in every shade and giant blocks of notepads and day planners. Once my box is complete, I will never be lost for an envelope again. More importantly, any craft project I need to do, I will do quickly and efficiently. I like having bits of cardboard around my room with photos and motivational phrases on them. On my desk right now, there is a picture of Yoko Ono wearing a cool hat and a quote from a weightlifting magazine: *DO NOT CHEAT DO NOT QUIT* – just like that, no punctuation or anything. I don't know if these things do me any good, but what I do know is it took me twenty minutes to find the scissors to cut them out, and a bus trip to gather the coloured card I glued them onto. I could have spent that time more wisely. Making soup and freezing it, or learning Arabic, or at least sourcing some more inspirational messages.

With this box, though, no more wasted time. I will be a ruthless provider of bits and pieces. You're stuck for a pen, with a nice nib, in black? Step inside, take your pick – there are thirty to choose from. You need a card saying, *Welcome to the world, twin girls*, with a photo on it of two kittens in pink ribbons nuzzling each other? No problemo. You want the novelty-sized one or the normal sized? You want to post it, within Ireland or abroad? Belfast? International stamp, it's all yours.

What if the ink runs out of the printer? Stop right there – shut up! It just won't. It will never run out, because I'll have thought of that and bought loads of cartridges and be in the glorious position of never again having to beg the hotel down the street to print out the carbohydrate content of vegetables. I will laugh in a carefree way when you need batteries, even small flat round ones, and then lead you by the hand to my stationery box. Because although batteries are not stationery, I will stock them too.

Following on from the stationery box, my ultimate fantasy, which I hope to achieve in the next decade, is to have a cupboard full of perfectly wrapped gifts appropriate for any occasion. For weddings of people I care about, there will be thoughtful, bespoke gifts, like photos in pearly frames of their children in sepia tones. For other weddings, I'll have piles of that Newbridge silverware stuff. I will be calm and prepared for birthdays. Other gifts too, for other reasons. You returned my turban, dear taxi man? Here is a scented candle for your trouble.

For now, though, I must focus on getting that box and filling it with drawing pins, bubble wrap and ring binders. I know that when I close the lid of the completed box and get the hemline just right on The Garment, I will be unstoppable. My troubles will melt like goddamn lemon drops.

What do you miss the most?

If you find yourself in Dublin city with a few hours to kill, you could do a lot worse than pay a visit to the bog bodies in the National Library. It's a really cool exhibition. The bodies are from the Iron Age, and are thought to have been killed as human sacrifices. Their leathery skin and red hair are quite gruesome, but nothing you would baulk at if you've been to Tullamore on a sunny day.

There are four bog bodies, each in a separate case. When scientists poked around and did some tests, they could tell an awful lot about them – even though all that's left of one poor fellow is a torso, a grimace and a really cool haircut which, apparently, he had kept in place with hair gel. Hair gel made from resin and oil: you can still see it clearly, thousands of years later. He was a hipster in his twentys, with a mohawk.

When I first learned this, my heart took a tumble and my brain cracked open. Everything sped up and slowed down simultaneously. He was wearing hair gel when he died. *Hair gel!?* Suddenly it was just me and him, in the middle of nowhere. I was in a trance, overwhelmed by questions for him …

Did you do your hair like that to impress a girl? On the day you were killed, did you have any idea what was coming? Were you generally happy with how you looked, or forever sighing when you caught your reflection in a puddle in the woods? Were you very frightened, or did you have time to be? Was there some kind of wattle-and-daub barber shop in existence? Who killed you? Did you tip the girl who washed you hair or just the stylist? What do you miss the most?

Then a grey-haired woman with thick ankles started coughing near the arrowhead display. The sound wrenched me back to the museum, and back to the present. I thought dumbly: *She looks Dutch.* A museum guard stretched as he read the paper. One leg of his trousers shifted, revealing a strap of hairy white shin. I blinked, hard, and wondered if it was too early for lunch.

The usual?

There are thousands of ways you can be miserable at work. Think of all the people who work in advertising and try to convince themselves they're fulfilling their creativity by doing so, or the teachers who are allergic to children, or the structural engineers who are afraid of bridges. For one terrifying summer, I worked for a man who hated his job so much, he used to tremble with rage as he ... opened the shutters of his café each morning.

You flung this book down in surprise, I bet, but put your mind back together: you read right. This man was a café owner and baker. A job so pleasant that many of us daydream about it. Some of us even plan menus and ask about loans and stock up on cute aprons when they're on offer, and ... Well, it doesn't matter, because this man was living that dream and hating every minute of it. I waitressed in his café the summer I moved to Dublin. Let's call him Philip. (I don't want to give his real name and risk him coming after me with a pastry fork. I don't think he will ever read this – he is the type of man who thinks books written by women must be for women – but you never know.)

243

I used to go in early, before opening, to set up the tables and fill up the sugar bowls. Each day at 7.30 a.m., Philip would fume over his first task in the kitchen, which was to make six apple tarts. Being an angry baker seems incongruous to me, but he had it down. He would turn the radio right up – usually a current affairs show where callers were encouraged to blame others for their misfortunes. You know, people who ring in and say things like: *I seen a single mother in my estate getting a massive allowance to buy her young one a communion dress, and there's me with no conservatory.*

Philip would curse the callers and blast the presenter, sweating as he sat on a tiny stool and peeled apples furiously. I don't know why he chose the frailest little seat in the building. He had a room full of comfortable chairs, but he perched on this plastic number with buckled legs every single morning, shifting uncomfortably and scraping it along the tiles. He didn't make things easy for himself, or fun. Not once did he peel the skin off an apple in one go, then toss it over his shoulder and check which letter it resembled, in order to speculate about people whose names began with that letter and whether or not he would do them. He never bothered making rhubarb and strawberry tarts instead of apple. Even if he found his work repetitive, he could have recited NWA lyrics to himself, like the rest of us do when we're bored, instead of focusing on how much he absolutely resented peeling apples.

Philip's mood would darken further as he moved on to the pastry. Great clouds of white would emerge from the bowl as he pummelled the flour into the fat. *Light hands!* I would scream to myself (in Darina Allen's voice). *For the love of*

God, light hands! He'd rush over to the sink, and stand there drumming the draining board with his floury fingertips, as he waited for the tea cup to fill with water. He really did not have those damn twenty seconds to spare. He'd splash the water into the flour, mix it up and then put the ball of pastry into the fridge to rest. He detested the resting time, frantically checking his watch over the following thirty minutes and muttering *For fuck's sake* at each check.

The only part of the process he seemed to find tolerable was the assembly of the pie: securing the edges of the pastry together and making slits in the top for the pie to cook through. He probably enjoyed that because it involved pinching and slashing the pies. Then he'd fling them into the oven and slam the door. Twenty-five minutes later, he'd huff over, whack the switch down and whirl the pies across the counter to a wire rack. They were so pretty, stoically smiling up at him and sending their fresh-baked smell around the kitchen. Sometimes I saw him glare at them throughout the morning and it made me shiver a bit: he just couldn't wait to cut them up. Despite his aggressive baking style, the results were divine. The pastry was short and buttery, the apple sweet and firm. We always sold out before 4 p.m.

Being a baker might not be your idea of paradise – I know it's not as great as, say, being a professional butter taster, or the person who phones patients on the transplant list and says: *Guess what, buddy? An organ that we think will fit you has … become available!* The thing is, we can't all win the career lottery. We can't all grow up and work as a judge in global bonny baby competitions: futuristic ones where we travel around the globe, inspecting massive tournaments

245

where babies compete in categories including 'sounds they make' and 'cheek circumference'. We can't all retire from comedy at thirty to become Michael Fassbender's comfort wife. I'm sorry that I was too scared of Philip to tell him that sprinkling cinnamon and sugar on fruit is not hard labour: it's a day in the life of Amélie Poulain.

I was scared of him because I was only young. Though he was nicer to me than to the rest of the staff, because I was the only Irish girl working there at the time. He did shout at me once because I undercharged a thin, sad-looking loner with a violin case. Old Pensive-Skinny-Malink-le-Roux was exactly the type of man I used to fancy when I was nineteen, that's why I let him pay less than half price for his tuna and sweetcorn sandwich, and that's why I got roared at by Philip. Mamma's different now – if someone shouts at her, she walks. Also, when it comes to men, Mamma wants athletes, please, and hold the introspection!

One shouting-at was bearable, compared to how he treated the others. He didn't bother learning the names of any of his foreign employees. Instead he called them by their country of birth. He'd say things like: *Tell Lithuania to clear table four straightaway.* And: *Brazil! I won't tell you again – you are NOT allowed to take milk with your lunch, unless you pay for it.* He did, however, call both Chinese waitresses Mary, and the Chinese washing-up man Paddy. That was his idea of a funny joke. Comedy is so subjective, isn't it?

When we were on our break together, I asked one of the Marys what her name really was, and she said it was Mary. I said: *No, I mean your real name*, and she said: *Flower*, and I said: *No, your Chinese name.* And again, she said: *Flower*, and got quite huffy. She told me that she didn't know why Irish people never believed her when she told them her name. Then she told me that my name in Mandarin means 'the man that is married to my sister'. She showed me a photo of her sister in her wallet, and I said I totally would and jiggled my eyebrows up and down. We had a good old laugh, and I was sorry later that afternoon when she cut her finger and got fired for bleeding on the chicken.

I got more scared of and fascinated by Philip as time went on. The other waitresses and I would speculate as to what was going on in his personal life that made him so rotten at work. Whatever it was, he carried it with him like a sack of rocks throughout the day in his busy, sunshine-filled café.

He lived for the moment someone would try to steal something from him. One morning he chased a woman into the street and wrestled with her to get back a banana she had hidden up her sleeve. Even though he got the banana back and terrified the woman, he called the Gardai. Two of them listened politely, as he ranted about how his business, family and health were: *in clear and present danger from people like her, on top of the fucking price of rent in the city centre.*

Despite my boss, I liked working there because it felt like an adventure. Look at me now, Mother, waiting on tables in one of the hippest cities in Ireland! There I was, in the Big Smoke, making sandwiches for tourists and businessmen and even some musicians! In 2001, Dublin was just waking up to the possibility that we could be rich *and* Irish, and also waking up to a new type of bread roll called a 'bagel'. Of the two possible futures, only bagels have gone the distance – though they seemed so far-fetched in the beginning. Breathless exchanges took place over lunch breaks: *Did you hear they are boiled? What you do is, you toast them and put cream cheese on them, not like other bread rolls. They are like magic. They are from America!*

We served bagels in the café and I delighted in talking to my sisters on the phone and saying things casually, like: *When you come up to visit, I'll take you to my café and we can get a bagel or something* … I'd leave a beat for the confused pause, and jump in to explain the phenomenon, then wipe the floor with them, by adding: *If you don't like the sound of bagels, we can just grab a panini.*

In the months I worked there, something changed. Sandwiches suddenly took on individual identities. Instead of a toasted ham-and-cheese sandwich, customers had to ask for a Liffey Laugher Special. Little did I know that was only the beginning of a phoney new intimacy between victuallers and their customers. Now, just over a decade later, when you buy a cup of coffee, you cannot escape without knowing the name of everyone involved in its creation. There's a name badge on the barista and a shout-out to the farmer on the blackboard behind the till. As you wait for your latte, the man who cleans the milking machines is personally introduced to you, while the cup manufacturer waves you off and Louis Pasteur himself gives you the thumbs-up as you walk past the window. I miss the olden days of identical, anonymous coffee shops, where you could drop dead and nobody would press a loyalty card with a content-looking cow into your frozen hand.

I liked working behind the sandwich bar that also was part of the café. I always tried to bear in mind the sandwich I was ultimately making, and not just pile fillings into bread in any old ratio. Who wants more semi-sundried tomatoes than turkey? Nobody! It annoys me when sandwich makers clearly don't care about what they're doing. I watch them throwing too much roast beef and not enough mustard onto bread that hasn't been buttered properly, the meat hanging out any which way, with no thought to the person who'll later be trying to eat it on the tram. They fail to distribute the lettuce evenly, and they skimp on the relish. That said, it is difficult to make an effort with someone's sandwich when they clearly care very little about it themselves. I came across people all the time, who just slumped against the counter and said crushing things like: *Just lob a bit of coleslaw on top of whatever cheese you have* – or the horrifyingly straightforward: *Can I get potato salad and stuffing in a white roll, please?*

Thankfully, most people did care about their lunch. I had a kind of game with some of the better regulars, especially this one bald man with glasses who worked in the Department of Finance. He used to order something different every day. He and I would play around with words while I made his lunch. *A whisper of peppers?* I'd ask him.

Go for it, but really just infer them on there, I don't want them overpowering the corned beef.

No problem, the corned beef can be bashful alright, so I'll just insinuate them on there.

I'll take a hefty dose of tomatoes too: I'm after a motherload of that lycopene today.

Moving on to mayonnaise, you want a mega-daub or just a touch-up?

I don't remember how it started, but it used to make my day. I miss Old Gogglebox-No-Hair-Great-Vocabulary-Le-Roux.

My favourite thing was recognising people and asking them if they wanted *the usual*. I suspect the flattery of that put undue pressure on people to just say yes, even if they were planning on ordering something else. Also, in my heart of hearts, I know that I used to sometimes forget what people liked, and rather than ruin the moment, I'd wing it from memory. I relied on the fact that they were too polite to correct me, as I used feta instead of goat's cheese, or sprinkled their bagel with capers they would have to carefully extract when they were back at their desks. Someone knowing your 'usual' is just such a lovely idea that we all went along with it.

Here is a tip from me to any of you working in the food industry: you can make someone's day, simply by repeating something back to them that they've previously told you about themselves. You know, along the lines of this: *Cheryl, hi! Hope the gastric bypass is working out well. Do you want me to liquidise the lemon meringue pie you like straight into the chowder, to save you some time? I know you've got the big meeting with Ernst & Young to prepare for!*

I suppose it's like a small-scale version of that thing where a man creates a memory box for a woman, full of miscellaneous crap she's talked about down through the years – her favourite childhood sweets, a bottle of discontinued perfume, and music from an ad she once mentioned she liked. Though I am deeply suspicious of people who remember small things

I've said. I feel like they've been studying me, and what am I – a set of blueprints? No! I am a regular human girl. I contradict myself a lot and cannot remember most of what I've said in the past. From one day to the next, I don't even know if I like truffle oil and, five years later, the jury remains out on Bon Iver.* Anyway, the point is that in the courtroom of my life, I am an unreliable witness. It's important that you stop paying attention to what I say, except for this one thing. This is what I know for sure. Even if you're Philip, if you get to wake up in Dublin city on a summer morning, and you've got some place to be and something to do, you should be delighted with yourself. You should at least start out happy, because when it comes down to it, your life is as easy as pie.

---

* His song about kissing outside a blood bank is great, but why does he always go on about living in a cabin? So what? Everybody wears those stupid check shirts. And did he ever actually fight a bear? I doubt it.

You sit right there,
Mamacita

The best taxi journey I've ever made began when I sat into a mint-green Mercedes on Dame Street on a Thursday afternoon. I was going to walk up to the rank opposite the bank, but it was absolutely metres away and I was exhausted. I had just had blood tests done and although the doctor only took a tiny amount, I always feel like any needling, however slight, is a big achievement.

You should see me after I've actually donated blood – I become the child in *The Secret Garden*. Not the feisty girl – I mean the snivelling boy. I whimper to the nurses and squirrel away the Bourbon Creams before I take myself home to the chaise longue. There I sit quietly, hoping a bruise will develop so I can show it to people and they can see how I generously contribute to society. Not only with my important art (prank shows, jokes about my mother), but with my actual blood.

Imagine that: I give my blood to strangers! What a woman. I don't even care who gets it. In an ideal world, my blood would always be transfused to a cute baby or to a hunk in need, but of course you can't dictate where it ends up. In yet another act of civic generosity, I would like to state that I wouldn't even mind if my blood went to bad people. A bicycle thief, who'd cut his hand on the job? Let him live, Doctor: proceed with the transfusion. A burlesque performer, who'd cracked her head open clambering out of a colossal shell? No way. Sorry, Miss Stupid-Tassles-Le-Roux, but I'm going to pour it down the drain instead.

That afternoon in the taxi, I wasn't just being dramatic: I was truly wrecked. I was tired because of my newly diagnosed ticker problem, and also tired from coming up with ways of describing how tired I was. I'd phone my sister Lilly and say: *I feel like I've been hit by a train and the driver forgot to kiss his wife, and so he went back home and hit me again on the way and then was late, so hit me super-hard the third time.* Or I'd catch Raedi as she tried to get upstairs and away from me (I only climbed the stairs in emergencies when I was sick, she knew this), and I'd call weakly: *Hey you, I feel so tired – like I've got the world on my shoulders and also Jupiter, which is the biggest planet in our solar system. Maybe I should take it easy.*

It didn't start out as a promising journey. The driver was talking into a headset in an African language that I didn't understand. If it had been Shona and he was saying *Good morning,* I would have completely got it because I learned how to say *Mangwanani* when I was in school in Zimbabwe. You must understand though that there are literally dozens of languages used in Africa and even more words, so I couldn't make out what he was on about.

Anyway, I told this driver where I was going and he headed off in the right – but long way around – direction. I tapped him on the shoulder to let him know I wanted him to do a U-turn. I didn't want to interrupt his call, so I just drew a circle in the air and sort of grimaced. He looked at me in the mirror and finished up his phone call by saying something, I'd imagine, like: *Uh-oh, I've got a live one – better go before she soils the car.*

Then he asked: *Are you OK, my lady?*

I warmed to him at once. *My lady*, if you will. I certainly will! A taxi driver in New York called me *Mamacita* once. His exact words were: *You sit right there, Mamacita.* Well, I died and went to heaven. *My lady* was definitely a close second. I appreciated the respectfulness of it and felt my shoulders lift back a bit and my face become steely but generous. You know that look? I do it with a little smile, which says to my shivering subjects: *Do not fear – simply bow to my will and all will be well. Your Lady shall give you enough bread to fill your bellies and enough coal to fill your hearths.*

Anyway, I told him I was fine but that I needed him to do a U-turn. I explained it was quicker that way and he said: *It's also illegal.* But he did put his indicator on.

I said: *I'm willing to take the rap – I'll tell the Gardai I made you do it. You can stay with your wife and kids: I'll go to jail for this.* He shook his head, but was smiling a tiny bit. *I'm telling you*, I said. *I'll do the time – you have my word.*

He said: *OK, that's OK, but I don't know how you would like it in jail.*

I'd like it just fine, I know it well enough – I'm only just out of there.

I was thinking you look like a tough woman, he replied.

I am. I won't even tell you why I was there in the first place: you would be too terrified.

And we were off! He bit his lower lip and gripped the

wheel with his arms straight out and his hands trembling. He said: *I am already terrified, my lady, a tough woman with her shades on, just out of prison and in my car – and I have no weapon!*

You'll be fine, just keep your eyes on the road. I'm wearing these shades for a reason. People can tell when they look in my eyes that I'm a total psychopath, and I don't want to give them any warning before I cut them up.

Ooof! he said, and we both burst out laughing. There was silence then for a moment as we stopped at the lights. A Garda car pulled up next to us. The taxi man looked over his shoulder at me, as I slumped down the seat a bit and put my hand up to cover the side of my face.

Are they looking at me? I asked him.

He put his hand up to the side of his face too, and theatrically peeped through his fingers: *Yes, they are, and they seem very frightened.*

Good, I said. *They're clever boys. Not like the others.* I paused for effect.

He said in a low, pleading tone: *Please tell me – have you ever killed a taxi driver?*

ARE YOU WEARING A WIRE? I screamed, and then we both lost it again. Then I told him he could relax, if he got me home and didn't tell anyone he'd seen me. I said I'd let him live, adding: *Unlike the guy on the bus that morning: I did the opposite of let him live.*

He ran with this. *There was another person on your bus? What was he – a suicide man? That is crazy behaviour. We all know that bus is your bus. His mother was a fool to let him grow up and never learn that.*

I know. Well, she's lost her son because of it – I hope she's learned her lesson.

We had reached my house. As I counted out the fare, he said in a stagey whisper: *Please allow me to say how grateful I am to you – my family will be so happy that you let me survive. I cannot believe it!*

You're not out of the woods yet, taxi man! I bellowed. He jumped. I got out of the car slowly. He covered his face with his hands. I wrapped things up with a menacing *Anyone asks? You never saw me.*

No, no, never, thank you – thank you so much. He drove off, still crouched in his seat, beeping goodbye as I shuffled into the house.

My fiancé will close proceedings

Get ready to take your suicide pills, men of the world! I have an announcement. I don't want to get married. This from a girl who a) hasn't been asked, and b) spent the winter of 2006 dressed in a wedding dress asking men to marry her for a TV prank show. So you can be certain I know what I'm talking about. In my own sweet time, I will settle down with someone and do all of that husband-and-wife stuff. Oh, I'll tell the lucky man all my plans, I'll support him in the Ironman races he regularly competes in, and I'll criticise him for not washing the floor the right way (my way). I just don't want a wedding.

Lots of weddings are romantic and fun. Lots more are mechanical and tedious. Living together and loving each other until we snuff it? Yes, please. I'll just skip the cold church, the meaningless music, the going-through-the-motions, the old family animosities papered over for an evening, the rapid weight loss, the giant debt, the kooky venue, the drunken singing, the bolero cardigans – and the proposal that sets the whole machine off.

That's really what it comes down to: I do not want a proposal. My aversion to proposals comes largely from listening to men describe how they proposed to their fiancées, and expecting me to fall a little bit in love with them for it. The amount of trouble they've gone to correlates directly with the number of times they repeat the story, so that we can all know how wonderfully inventive and terribly cute they are. In the retelling of a proposal, no detail is too small: each little twist is a worthy point to *ooh* and *aah* over. It is the engaged woman's role to reinforce the tale gently from the sidelines.

A typical anecdote tips along something like this:

John: *See, Ellen loves McDonald's McMuffins, yeah?*

Ellen, beaming: *Yeah, they're my favourite breakfast when I'm hung over some weekends.*

John picks it up again: *Some weekends? Ah, more like, every single Saturday and Sunday morning, you bloody alco – and you mill into them! Anyway, this was on Sunday and we were both locked after the match on Saturday, so I knew she'd want her double sausage and egg McMuffin meal, so I got into the car ... and I totally shouldn't have, because I was definitely still over the limit ... How much did we drink that night?*

Ellen: *Oh I don't know, Jesus. Shit-loads anyway.*

John: *Yeah, but I was like, fuck it – you have the ring, today is the day, just go for it. And it was fine, didn't get stopped, just hit the Drive-Thru out on the Naas Road and got home before she even woke up. That was perfect, because it gave me time to set the whole thing up on the coffee table.*

Ellen: *Oh, you should have seen it – it was unreal, he made a smiley face out of —*

John: *Ellen, you do a shit job of describing it, I'll tell her! OK, so – what I did was, I tore up one sausage patty to make the eyes and used the bun as ears, then I smeared the egg into a big grinning mouth kind of shape. I did a heart-shaped speech bubble with salt and it took me eleven sachets of ketchup to write MARRY ME inside it. I was calling her for ages to come down but she took so long …*

Ellen: *I thought he was joking at first, 'cos I didn't really know what was going on – it was so early, I suppose.*

John: *She kept saying: 'What is that? Who is that supposed to be? Is that me?' And in the end I was like, no, you spa, that's supposed to be me, asking you to marry me! And I sat her down and gave her the coffee that comes with the meal deal, 'cos I needed her to drink that to finish my plan!*

Ellen: *I was just speechless.*

John: *For once in your life! Have you ever seen this girl with nothing to say? It was incredible. I kept encouraging her to drink more, but you know the way that coffee is always way too hot – it was taking her ages to finish it.*

Ellen: *I kind of scalded my throat alright.*

John: *But eventually she started coughing and thumping her chest, so I knew she'd reached the ring – see, I'd dropped the ring into it! She had no clue, but then she brought it up and realised what it was!*

Ellen, looking at John adoringly: *I think I was sick from shock as much as from choking on the ring, though – I had no idea he was planning all of this. I really did get the surprise of my life.*

John sits back, arms folded, confident that their beautiful story has melted one more heart. Ellen, rubbing his arm: *I couldn't even eat the McMuffin after all of that! And I actually do love them.*

John: *But sure, it was cold at that stage anyway.*
Ellen: *Well, that's true.*

Listen John, it's nice that you registered on some level a key part of Ellen's personality – it's lovely that you made a romantic effort and wonderful of you to support a local business. But don't expect me to collapse in a heap of admiration and envy. I am and will remain sullen on the matter, thank you.

The only time I'd waive my ban and allow someone to propose to me would be on my deathbed. Don't you think it such a nice – if ultimately empty – gesture? For a man to propose to a woman, who has only a week or so left in her? Yes, I would go along with that. It's just so romantic!

Also, importantly, it would give me something to focus on other than my own demise. I would drag myself out of the hospice for dress fittings and even if I had some terrible wasting disease, it wouldn't matter. The dressmakers would hardly bat an eyelid at my shrinking frame, because that's what brides do anyway. I would go bravely to the florist's and cough weakly from a wicker wheelchair to indicate my preferences: once for roses, twice for carnations.

I would make sure to die before the wedding day, to save money. That would also ensure that my funeral would have to incorporate a number of heart-wrenching references to what might have been. Here is how I see it going down – touch wood:

The priest will focus on how great I was, as is customary. He will also refer to how happy I was to have got engaged at last, and he'll make people sob with talk of me whispering to him, as he gave me the last rites: *I … just … want … to*

... *be ... a ... Bride*. The flower girls will wear black puffball dresses and make sad faces, as they scatter lily petals up the aisle. My little stiff hand (complete with French manicure) will bear a simple diamond ring.

Naturally, I will be buried in a wedding dress with my hair in a not overly severe chignon, and the mortician will set my face into a blissful smile. I think the dress will be mermaid-style, bordering on fully fish-tail. It will need sleeves, so that I can have that V-shaped part that comes out of the sleeve and around the middle finger, though that might make the whole look a little too busy. We'll see. I will definitely have a veil, one that my tearful fiancé will lower, just before they clamp the lid on the coffin. I am imagining an ivory-coloured coffin, with stencilled images of cherubs flying towards the heavens on the backs of a couple of swans.

The speeches will be real tearjerkers. All going to plan, my father will set a dignified but devastated tone. He will let slip that I was indeed his favourite child. My sisters, wearing their strapless lemon-coloured bridesmaids' dresses with black sashes, will smart for a second, then feel guilty and go back to wailing. My fiancé will close the proceedings, his voice trembling. He'll manage to keep it together just long enough to tell everyone I was a genius in the kitchen, a humdinger in the living room, an absolute firecracker in the bedroom, and an able washerwoman in the utility room. He may well finish up with: *And now, surely, she is a beautiful angel in heaven.*

Then he'll collapse at the unfairness of me not being alive on My Big Special Day. He'll have to hop up again, though! Because I will have left strict instructions for him to carry my coffin alone, in order to heighten the sadness of the occassion. It will be a physical struggle, I'd imagine – but if he loves me enough to want me as his wife, he'll love me enough to come up with a system of ropes and pulleys to get my boxed-up body from the altar to the graveyard.

How I want my stuff to be divvied out

One day, I was home on my own watching *America's Next Top Model*. As the show ended and the latest girl to be booted out faded from the group photo, I thought to myself: *I should make a will*.

The things that are most important to me cannot be doled out like sweets; I'm talking about my family. OF COURSE. Who wouldn't love a big group of brown-haired people who know you very well, yet still insist on loving you? And also, I couldn't possibly give away my friends. I don't even like sharing my friends when I'm alive. If I notice one of them having their head turned by a new person, I do all I can to undermine the new person. I plant seeds of doubt about their characters, with vague accusations: *Isn't he a bit old to still call people 'dude'?* Or: *I don't know, she just seems like she doesn't really get it, you know?* I'm terrible that way. Enough about me as a person now: what is a person anyway, but a collection of possessions?

Here is how I want my stuff to be divvied out.

My Clothes

Right now I own two pairs of trousers. Blue jeans and black jeans: I am basically Billy Ray Cyrus. I have some nice dresses, and they will go to my local charity shop with strict instructions to hide them when Raedi pops in. Not that I expect them to remain on the hangers for long. You'd be surprised how in demand flowery dresses from Penneys are – or maybe you wouldn't.

I have an odd assortment of shoes, literally and aesthetically. After a particularly disorganised tour of Australia in 2008, I returned home with five single shoes, their twins left under hotel beds or backstage in a theatre in some godforsaken place like Townsville. I felt guilty about throwing out the remaining shoes, even though they really were useless. I had a vague plan to use them as quirky plant pots. However, a geranium sticking out of a woman's boot isn't so much: *Aren't I cute and inventive? Feel my whimsy through the medium of shoe plant pots!* – as: *Look! I murdered a lady and stole her shoes for my crazy-garden.*

I am blessed with broad feet. For my birthday Raedi gave me a pair of canvas shoes with navy and white stripes on them. She knows that horizontal stripes don't do any broad parts any favours, yet she went ahead and chose these, over a pair of slimming black pumps, say, or discreetly tight loafers. It's funny how you think you know someone, and then they twist the knife like that, isn't it? In any case, I bequeath those stripy shoes, my furry boots and my flip-flops to any woman with size 6½, extra-wide-fit feet who thinks she can handle them.

I'm sure you're applauding my generosity, but you're also probably thinking: *Hang on, Maeve – it's all well and good for you to give away your clothes, but what will you wear in your coffin?* I've thought about that and I'd actually like to get something new for my funeral. I want to be buried in the fashion of the day. I'm planning on making my coffin something of a time capsule, so that if it's dug up and examined by archaeologists in ten years or so, they will marvel at how we lived today. I am planning an authentic, fascinating selection of things that play a part in our daily lives. So far, I have two low-carb diet books, a Lidl receipt and a Kardashian.

And what a treat – to be bang on trend for the first time in my life! Technically I won't still be in my life, but I repeat, what a treat! To ensure my look is as fashionable and up-to-date as possible, I will leave instructions for my heartbroken sisters to scan fashion magazines and search through celebrity websites. They will be able to collate information from all of those pieces where there are rows of photos of famous women in nice dresses with '✓' or '✗' scribbled beside their outfits. The headline is usually something like: *What was this asshole bitch thinking?* Or: *How the fuck dare she think she can wear this?* Then my sisters can commission a dress for me, combining all of the elements approved of by the fashion journalists. Mark my words: I will have an impact on the fashion world, in this life or the next.

My Discman and CDs

I have a real problem figuring out the technology that would allow me to get music I like to go into my ears when I want it to. I have a number of listening devices that my best friend Ian loads up with music for me, but they often just sit blinking at me, and no matter how many screens I touch, or buttons I press, they remain totally silent. So I snuck into Argos one day last year and bought a Discman. I will leave it to Ian. It's kind of a passive-aggressive gesture, but he won't mind.

My Extensive Collection of Dental Floss and Picks

Although these are an important and pleasurable part of my life, I understand that they are of little value to anybody else, so I am fine about them being thrown into the bin.

My Money/Debts

Depending on what time of year I depart this world, my bank account might be full or it might be empty. My life is like that of a seasonal fruit picker, financially at least – I do have basic rights and don't do half as much manual labour as them. What if I die in the midst of owing a load of money to my phone company? Let's say, for example, I had not realised there was no wi-fi on the bus one day and had run up a gigantic bill by downloading Sophia Grace and Rosie videos for three hours, then what? Then my parents would have to pay, I suppose.

Hopefully, it won't come to that. Hopefully, my hunch is correct, and I am actually immortal. Failing that, maybe I'll die rich. If so, I will leave €100 to each of my dear siblings and tell them to go wild in their bakery of choice. Ideally, I would love to leave a tonne of money to good causes. Not anonymously – I don't understand people who do that. If you've gone to all the hassle of earning money and you've resisted spending it on juice machines and silver earrings, and you then hand it over to some needy strangers, at least take your praise. Take it with you, wherever the hell you're going.

My Desk

I bought my desk in 2001. It is a light oak kitchen table from Habitat. It has a few tea stains on it, and a mark from where I left a cheap lamp burning for too long. For years, my desk was nothing more than an aspirational piece of furniture, covered in unopened bills and scribbled ideas I had yet to follow through. Now, I see it more as a colleague with whom I have a mutually beneficial type of relationship. If I keep boring paperwork in a respectable pile in one corner and don't crowd him with bottles and used teacups, if I spend a few hours sitting with him every morning, my desk responds by being steady and focused.

I am pleased that I have fixed up our relationship to the point that I now write at my desk. That, more than anything, makes me think I must be a writer. I've got to be. Why else would this desk willingly allow me to sit and write at it, wearing whatever the hell I want? I genuinely seem to be a writer. I'm sure I am. And that makes me unbelievably happy. Happier, even, than when I'm mixing Minstrels into popcorn at the cinema, and there's a great guy with his arm around me who understands that if he wants Minstrels and popcorn of his own, he should just buy them and not try and take mine. I am happy being selfish and I am selfish with this happiness, and with this desk that contributes so much towards it. I don't want any other clown writing their try-hard stuff all over him. So, I will leave my desk to my father, who loves to chop big pieces of wood into small pieces of wood and burn them.

Little Edie

It's as hard to give a cat away as it is to own one, and Little Edie is no different in this respect. She will do as she wishes. I suspect that will involve my neighbour, but will not be drawn on the subject. I will of course organise a trust fund for Little Edie, although that may attract the wrong type of tomcat to her. The gold-digging type. I will have to put some conditions on the money. I must phone my solicitor at once. I bid you *Adieu*.

Acknowledgements

Some of the ideas in this book came from diary pieces for RTÉ Radio 1 and columns for the *Irish Independent* and *Irish Times*, many thanks to the editors for permission to use them here.

I'd like to thank the following people, who did all sorts of amazing things to help me write this book – Claudia O'Doherty, Seán Reid, Faith O'Grady, Aoife Naughton, Eugene Mirman, Alan Bennett, Ian Cudmore, Niamh Tiernan, Maureen Concannon, Lauren Hadden, Cathal Murray, Yvonne Hogan, Richard Cook and Ciara Considine.

Finally, huge thanks to my parents and all The Sisties – including Oliver, with a special shout out to my girl Raedi Higgins.